KNIGHT OF
THE WHISTLE

The life of pioneer
Ralph Tarrant

Ralph Tarratt

as told to Phil Dennett and Jeremy Gambrill

First published in October 2003 by Whistleblower
ISBN Number 09513590-1-0
Copyright © Philip Dennett 2003

A CIP catalogue record for this book is available from the British Library.

Printed by Sherlock Printing, Bolney Grange Business Park, near Burgess Hill, Sussex

In memory of Edith Tarratt, Joy Tarratt, Dorothy Thomas, Arthur Dennett and Jeremy Gambrill, who all faced cancer with great courage

CONTENTS

FOREWORD

As an ex-footballer who passed his refereeing examinations I have some sympathy with the "man in the middle."

So I am delighted to recommend Knight of the Whistle and I hope that it raises thousands of pounds to help people with cancer, as Ralph Tarratt intended of course when he decided to get this book written.

In the late 40s and early 50s Ralph and I were both making our different ways in football.

Our paths crossed as his refereeing career took him to games at Brentford and Fulham, where I was playing in that exciting period when huge crowds supported football.

Much later in life I met his family when we became involved in fund-raising to help people with cancer.

One of the many programmes Ralph has kept shows him refereeing a game on 10 November 1951 at Upton Park when I played left-half (anyone remember them?) and alongside me in the Brentford half-back line was a certain Ron Greenwood.

Reporters noted the game drew only 26,500 for a Second Division match, an indication of the large crowds that were usually drawn to football in those days.

Ralph refereed in an era of wonderful players like Lawton, Matthews, Carey, and Mercer, to name just a few.

At grass roots level he pioneered the way for Sussex referees to achieve great success outside the county, and of course his name is still known widely for the bar billiards business he started in Sussex.

His story is one of warmth and humour and I wish him every success with his book.

Jimmy Hill Hurstpierpoint West Sussex 2003

INTRODUCTION

When Ralph Tarratt broke his arm a few years ago in his late 80s at his home in Southwater, near Horsham, West Sussex, the first thing he instinctively reached for to call for help was his old Acme Thunderer referee's whistle, which he kept with him for such emergencies.

Nothing could have been more apt for Ralph, because the whistle has played a huge part in his life and in that of those around him.

Ralph was the first referee from Sussex to reach the First Division, which was then the top flight of football. Before then the county's referees were outcasts, stuck in a football outback. Armed with a whistle and notebook, strong determination, and a fair degree of charm, he took the county's men in black out of the shadows and into national recognition.

Ralph is in the elite band of only six referees from Sussex since the game began to reach the top flight. He also reached the top of the county's football management as chairman of the Sussex County FA from 1961-62. As a former referee Ralph was delighted when the vastly experienced League and international referee Martin Bodenham, one of the few from the county to reach top level, was appointed the first-ever Head of Refereeing for the Sussex County FA in 2001, building on what Ralph had started so many years before. When Bodenham told Brian Owen of the Evening Argus upon his appointment that the County F.A. would help any referees with potential through the ranks, it echoed Ralph's attitude to aspiring referees five decades ago. Martin told me in October 2003, while I was researching this book: "Ralph was a very highly respected referee in his time."

Ralph also made football history, and created one of the biggest national sports stories of the time, by sending off former Arsenal idol Ronnie Rooke, the first time a player-manager had suffered such an indignity. At the same time as his career progressed he injected some vigour into local refereeing, even introducing a Continental flavour to the market town of Horsham by attracting a top speaker from Portugal for a local meeting because of his international connections.

During his career Ralph acquired the title in some quarters of Knight of the Whistle, for the courteous and fair way he tried to treat all those he came across in the game, although as people recall later in this book there has always been an edge of steel about him when needed.

Ralph handled many matches for Brighton and Hove Albion, including thrilling league games, benefit matches and friendlies. When Albion played Czech side Bank Ostrava Football Club on 13 March 1957 at the Goldstone Albion manager Billy Lane reminded thousands of people of Ralph's "title" when he wrote in the programme: "We thank the officials, Mr Ralph Tarratt, of Southwater, who is "Knight of the Whistle", Mr C Poulter of Hove and Mr J Daive, of Worthing, who officiate as linesmen."

Despite the respect that Ralph generally commanded, he once had a crowd of 160,000 baying for his blood in South America, where he also had to be locked in a dressing room after sending four players off in another game. His travels to South America also brought him face to face with the powerful Peron phenomena in Argentina.

At the highest domestic football level Ralph shared the football turf with legendary footballers like Tommy Lawton, Busby "Babe" Roger Byrne, Joe Mercer, Johnny Carey, Alf Ramsey, and John Charles during the hundreds of games he refereed between the mid 30s and the late 50s, often before huge and passionate crowds. He was at the heart of the biggest football boom ever to hit this country after the end of the Second World War, when crowds of up to 80,000 or more that have never been equalled packed into grounds every Saturday.

But Ralph also got as much joy from being in control of Sussex County League matches involving top local teams like Haywards Heath, Horsham, and Worthing. He even found himself refereeing before large sun-baked crowds during Army service abroad, and answered the call for numerous charity matches during his career.

In the early days, for those fervently fought glittering top Football League games he recalls he would get three pounds and three shillings, while for local matches like Rusper versus Crawley Athletic reserves in the 1930s he pocketed a mere two shillings and six pence. Talk to Ralph for a few minutes and you quickly see money could never have been the motivation, but clearly his love of the game and a certain determination to succeed. At the height of his career footballers, like referees, were relative paupers compared to some of the fantastic wages of £80,000 a week or more paid to today's stars like Beckham and Henry.

The poor pay of 50s footballers was a dreadful reward for drawing huge crowds and incomes for their clubs, and they were kept firmly in their place by infamous maximum wage regulations and contracts which reduced even the greatest stars like Stanley Matthews and Tom Finney to little more than serfdom. It is perhaps hard for people to believe in these days when players arrive for training in £50,000 cars, that in the 1930s, 1940s, and 1950s stars arrived for matches on the tram or bus and mingled with supporters. In many cases professional players in their precarious careers were earning little more than the factory and office workers who watched them, and this may have been the reason there was a closer bond in those days between players and crowds.

Ralph's long path to the top began with refereeing lower grade football in 1932, when he was only 22, after a football injury ended his days as a centre-forward in local football. It was not long before the West Sussex County Times weekly newspaper, which chronicled his path regularly throughout his career, called him "the young but well known referee." His lower league and top-flight days covered a period from the early 1930s to the mid-1950s when football was the nation's great live passion.

Like all referees he had to retire from top-level football in his 40s, but continued refereeing in junior football and charity games until he was 61 and became chairman of the Sussex County Referees Association. He also led the first board to run Horsham Football Club. His thick scrapbooks of memories are packed with cartoons, quotes, and profiles on refereeing that are testimony to his passion for the game of football. They have helped Ralph relive some of his finest moments on and off the pitch in this book.

Sharing in the glory game and keeping fascinating scrapbooks did not pay household bills and Ralph combined his dedication to refereeing with a successful business life. Look around the pubs and clubs in Sussex and you will still see Tarratt bar billiards and pool tables.

Ralph took the new game to the corners of Sussex more than 60 years ago, spreading it from its first base in the Horsham and Billingshurst area to other areas of the county. A Ralph Tarratt bar billiards trophy for Sussex singles is still played for nearly 40 years after it was first proudly won in season 1964-65 and pool leagues bear the Tarratt name. For example, the Mid Sussex Tarratt Pool league, centred ten miles from the Heath pub in Haywards Heath "as the crow flies" attracts about 50 teams for its main winter season and also runs another competition in the summer. It celebrates its 25th anniversary in 2004 and all but about five teams use Tarratt tables, the rest playing under special permission from Tarratts, who are sole sponsors.

The days of 20p a game bar billiards long disappeared with the 50 pence pint, but although no longer at a peak both pool and bar billiards still attract good support and players with high levels of skill. When bar billiards first emerged as a national pub and club game in the 1930s Ralph was at the forefront, touring pubs and collecting table "rents" and soon establishing his own firm and league. Ralph quickly saw that the game was attractive because it took up a relatively smaller space than some other table games. This was helped by the fact that players take their shots from a D at only one end of the table, unlike snooker, which requires space for shots to be taken from all around.

He also recognised that a game where players paid a fee to play for a finite amount of time, in England up to 19 minutes, was bound to have its financial attractions for pub and club owners, who would also enjoy a spin-off from bar sales, especially if leagues were formed with visiting teams. For some players there was the "mathematical" attraction of notching up great scores of 20,000 or more for top players in one single game of bar billiards. This is because until the time limit is reached and a wooden bar drops balls are always returned and available for scoring.

For some unexplained reason in Sussex until about ten years ago 20,000 scores were rare, but now there is a long list of players who have achieved it, with some scoring well beyond 20,000. They have a special bright red "20 K" shirt to remind them of their achievement, a scheme started by Steve Mariner and Julian Deeprose. One of the most remarkable performances since Ralph first introduced his tables was by the 1996 Sussex Open winner Mark Sawyer. He scored 29,000 in 17 minutes and 39 seconds in 1999 during the Oxford open.

In February 2002 at the Stadium Tavern in Hove Steve Mariner scored 27, 530, and there are plenty of other examples of extremely high scoring, including Chris Roe's 21,090 at Roundhill Tavern in Brighton in February 1993. The first 20,000 plus score nationally is reputed to be by 20-year-old Brian Hudson at Chatham on 3 January 1961, when he scored 22,100 in 19 minutes. Nowadays you can look up the rankings of players on a website. Paul Barnett was ranked only joint 158 in July 2003, but he took the Sussex County championship title, his first singles title. It was matter of great pride for Ralph when his own son

Rod took the Sussex singles title in 1970-71 followed by the Sussex Champion of Champions title.

Ralph's stepson from his second marriage to Edith, Mick Foskett, was a champion player himself. Ralph recalls that Mick once, free of charge, changed the timing clocks on hundreds of bar billiards tables when the price for a game went up. Ralph recalls Mick was an excellent player, good enough to play for Sussex, who could "play the table out".

Those unfamiliar with the game might like to know the name bar billiards is actually nothing to do with the fact that it is often played in public bars. The name relates to the wooden bar that drops automatically after a set time governed by a timing clock, stopping balls returning and signalling the closing stages of the game. It is said to be based on bagatelle, popular from the 1700s. In the 1930s an Englishman, David Gill, was in Belgium when he saw some men playing what was called Russian Billiards.

Using the maker that Ralph would later employ for his own tables, called Jelkes, Gill got a table of his own made and before long nearly 20 counties were playing, mostly in the South. On the table there are seven white balls and one red, and all shots are played from the end D into any of nine holes carrying different scores from 10 points to 2000. The major hazard of the game is avoiding knocking over either a white or a red skittle, which have fixed places on the table, while you are trying to reach the most lucrative holes.

It is bad enough knocking over the white skittle, which wipes out the scores you have made in your last turn, or "break" as it is known, and also hands the play to your opponent. But a terminal fate awaits if you hit the dreaded black skittle, the curse of the bar billiards player through the decades. Hit the black and you lose your entire score for the whole game, instantly handing victory to your opponent. Many a player has lost a game in this fashion while well in the lead with a score approaching 20,000 and it is this that gives the game its constant edge of excitement. The leading player is never quite safe until the clock drops the bar and the final ball is eventually played.

Ralph greatly enjoyed the day to day involvement as the original bar billiards agency and business evolved to meet new challenges, with the help later of his son Rod. Ralph was still helping in the business at the age of 78 and reached the position of chairman of the All-England Bar Billiards Association. From that first table at the Wheatsheaf pub in the village of Cuckfield, near Haywards Heath, Ralph's own firm grew and still thrives as Tarratt Tables under the management of Rod, although nowadays people have many counter-attractions.

Brighton and Hove Albion Football Club has also featured large in Ralph's life, through his involvement with refereeing first with reserve matches and then full league games, and Ralph maintained his interest in their fortunes after he hung up his whistle. Albion legends Johnny McNichol and Glen Wilson, cherished by a vastly different generation of supporters five decades ago, were familiar faces.

Ralph's memorable first senior game as a referee even created a little bit of Albion history on 19 August 1939. The team wore numbered shirts for the first time in that match against Crystal Palace at the now demolished and still lamented Goldstone Ground. They drew 3-3 in a pre-season friendly game before the outbreak of war in September threw the league into chaos and a battle for financial survival for the next six years. He watched Albion's fortunes plummet as the political situation wrecked the League structure. Gates for the doom-laden 1939-40 season veered from a best of 4,083 to the lowest of 450 on 8 June 1940, and debts of more than £5,000 took Albion close to liquidation.

Ralph says he always insisted that referees should not be "showy," but circumstances sometimes dictated that he reluctantly found himself at the centre of events. He tells in this book how a freak accident at a tension-packed Arsenal-Manchester United match led him to greater things. Ralph began taking Sussex

County League games in 1935, at the age of 25, which was remarkably young in the 1930s, then became the youngest ever linesman in the Football League.

He went on the Football League list in 1948 after war service and was the first Sussex referee ever to officiate at all three professional levels, taking Football League, Football Combination (reserve) Southern league as well as F.A.Cup matches. Ralph refereed in a time when spectators, even at top-level games, swayed on open rainswept terraces in grounds where facilities were by today's standards sometimes crude. But Saturday afternoon was their big shout of the week and they sent up a howls of support for their team and occasional spite for the referee.

Saturation football on television and television trial of referees was a long way off. The crowds enjoyed being judge and jury on the day and thrashing out their opinions in pubs and amongst friends instead of "ranting" into air on "phone-ins" to radio stations, in the remote fashion of the 21st century football follower.

In Knight of the Whistle Ralph, now 92 and living at the Ashtonleigh residential care home in Horsham, relives some of the highlights of his life and a few of the low points, including the heartbreaking end of his first marriage in wartime and the tragic loss of his second and third wives to cancer. Football is always at the heart of Ralph's story, which reminds us that every generation brings its own great footballers and indeed, great referees.

He also retains a great love of cricket, as a former member at the County Ground, Hove, and no one was happier when Sussex clinched their first County Championship title in September 2003. A photograph presented to him of Sussex skipper Chris Adams celebrating on the day is proudly on display in his room. As a former chairman of Southwater friends of St Catherine's Hospice at Crawley Ralph hopes sales of Knight of the Whistle will raise plenty of money for the charity and his family has paid for the production of the book to help towards that end.

On a personal note, I should like to pay tribute to the late Jeremy Gambrill, the co-author of this book. He undertook the project at a time when he was fighting the cancer that sadly took his life in 2002, with the book less than half-completed. I know Jeremy was anxious that this book should be finished both as a tribute to Ralph and to raise funds for St Catherine's.

Ralph lives in considerable discomfort from arthritis and has been in frail health, but he has cheerfully sat uncomplaining through many hours of taped interviews and note taking over about two years. He has little use of his hands but did his best with a struggle to write scribbled notes to help our research. His sheer determination to see this project through drove him to check every one of the 70,000-plus words, carefully scanning the book line by line with a large magnifying glass to help his weakened eyesight. It was no token gesture. Several changes were made as a result of his comments. Right up until the time we went to press late in 2003 Ralph has been still thinking up ideas, offering more stories, and checking we have covered the ground and had given due credit to other people.

Ralph's memories of local organisations go back to involvement with the Horsham YMCA club in his younger days, but he has also remained active in his later years. He recalls he was a founder member of the local Forest Probus branch at Horsham. In March 2003 he organised a highly successful Ralph Tarratt Charity Sports Dinner attended by Sussex captain Chris Adams, who was later to lead his team to the county championship that summer. About 100 others also enjoyed the dinner, at Southwater Cricket Club, which raised money for St Catherine's Hospice at Crawley and the Diabetic Retinopathy Screening Fund and Ralph has been busy planning another one for 2004.

Ralph's beaming smile, bright mind, and sense of humour convinced me his tales deserved to be told and Jeremy's work deserved to be finished, when I took over the researching and writing of Knight of the Whistle. On a point of style for readers, purely to help continuity some additional information from research about players and clubs other than that recalled personally by Ralph has been incorporated in Ralph's first person account, with his agreement.

On a personal note, it has been a pleasure to know Ralph and his family and I hope you enjoy reading his story as much as Jeremy and I enjoyed writing it.

By the way, to this day Ralph still keeps a whistle in a drawer in his bedroom.

Phil Dennett Burgess Hill October 2003

A WORD OR TWO FROM RALPH

I remember once hearing somebody say: "I look to the future because that is where I am going to spend the rest of my life."

I thought then it was a positive message and one to live by although now, at the grand old age of 92, my memories occupy more of my time than my plans for coming years, which is the way things ought to be. So I have wandered back through the years to recall some of the moments that have given me pleasure and which I hope may also make you smile.

Of course, life is not all laughs. There have been bad times and some of these have come bubbling to the top of my memory but, when I weigh the happy against the sad, the scales tip firmly toward those many, many times in my life when I have had cause to stop and be grateful for the life I have led

Over the years I have met some wonderful people and many of them are remembered in my book. Apologies to those I may have overlooked after so many years but I am sure you will also know the part you have played in my life and the joy you have brought, without a reminder from me.

The profits from this little book of mine are going to benefit people who badly need our help and I thank you for supporting them.

Ralph Tarratt Horsham October 2003

1   HIGHBURY   THE BIG BREAK

The famous old Highbury football ground was packed with 55, 451 captivated supporters as I sprinted down the muddy touchline in a gale and driving rain trying to watch the ball and the players at the same instant.

The mighty Arsenal were at home to Manchester United and, as Christmas 1951 neared, both were fighting for the League title. Turn the clock briefly forward 52 years and we see the same two proud clubs still fiercely disputing the modern day version of the League title, now called the Premiership.

In North London on that bleak December day ten decades ago the action was exciting enough to make the huge banks of shivering supporters who defied the downpour forget they were soaked, although Highbury's imposing stands at least offered more cover than most grounds in the 1950s. Now there are no teeming terraces and there is a smaller crowd at Highbury because everyone has to be seated. Top football in the raw has receded into the history books forever.

In that distant Saturday afternoon murk of half a century ago a new United began to light up the football world as they began to forge a new team playing with precision, dash, and passion. It was an exciting time for the Manchester lads and the fans and I was there at the dawn of it all. It was a day that would lead both United and me on a momentous path, although neither of us knew that at the time.

The newspaper reporters had just started to call some of the United players the Busby Babes after their manager Matt Busby began bringing in a new generation of talented young players. United had never been out of the top four since the war, had finished runners-up four times, and were desperate to win the title for the first time for 40 years when they arrived at Highbury. But when I looked at them coming out on to the pitch so confident before the game I saw this was no team of Babes.

Out there were some experienced and wily campaigners who knew all the tricks of the trade as far as professional football was concerned and the team was also packed with skill and imagination. For a start there was half-back Johnny Carey, getting on a bit then but one of the most polished, cool and versatile players ever to wear a United shirt and a man of impeccable behaviour even in the heat of battle. But there were two young players starting to bloom into greatness and both were to suffer in different ways in the Munich air crash in 1958.

At left-back United had Roger Byrne, who by the time of Munich was one of the most experienced players but when I saw him was a promising young player just making his way to greatness. Actually, I did not pick him out as being especially brilliant that day but there was a speed and boldness about him that made him look like a great one for the future. Of course he went on to play lovely football for England, a most elegant and composed full-back who later made a perfect captain for Busby's crusading European team until his terrible death in the air crash.

Also on good form that day was dashing winger John Berry, who gave Arsenal a torrid time. Many years later, soon after the Munich crash, I read that he had survived that terrible ordeal, but the sadness for him and all football fans was that he was never the same player again. All that Munich gloom was seven years away on that wonderful optimistic day when Matt Busby led out United.

But classy and crafty Arsenal, as was to be the case so many times afterwards, were to be United's challengers until the last day of the season, and this mid-season match on 8 December 1951 was a key game. Arsenal were unbeaten at home and were determined to stay that way. I was happy enough on such a marvellous occasion, soaked in tension among the players and anticipation among the supporters, to start as the senior linesman at the age of 41.

It was a responsible enough job in the heated atmosphere of Highbury, but sensational events were to unfold for me later. After 14 minutes United were leading 1-0 thanks to a fine volley from their wonderful striker Jack Rowley. It was the supreme Rowley's 20th goal of the season, from United's first serious attack. Arsenal could not say they had not been warned because the papers had reported in September that Rowley had already scored three hat-tricks in the first seven games of the season, which I think was a record at the time.

Although obviously I could not dwell on it at the time, it is wonderful to recall now that I was sharing the pitch, albeit at that precise moment from the touchline, with giants of football and the formidable Rowley was just one of them striding the historic Highbury turf. It seems to me that passing years acknowledge greatness more easily than the present, but Rowley's record stood against the best in a hard business.

In that season Rowley, who died in June 1998 at the age of 79, would hit 30 goals to help United to the League Championship. In his long and glorious United career from 1937 to 1955 he hit more than 200 goals including two in United's famous 4-2 FA Cup Final victory over Blackpool in 1948, judged to be one of the best in history, and he played six times for England.

Amusingly Rowley's fierce shooting both as a footballer and in war service as an anti-tank gunner earned him the nickname "The Gunner" from United fans, almost the same as Arsenal's famous nickname from their Woolwich Arsenal days. But from what I could glean in this important football afternoon in North London to my mind it was Arsenal's Gunners who were dominating the play on a mud bath of a pitch.

That slippery pitch was to play a dramatic and totally unexpected part in my progress as a Division 1 referee. After about ten minutes Doug Lishman,

Arsenal's slim and skilful inside-left, had spun away to slip his marker, lost his footing and his boot went sliding down the unguarded shin of the referee, Mr Law. The two of them fell to the floor in the middle of the pitch and clearly Mr. Law had taken quite a knock.

The trainers from both teams rushed on to attend the two casualties and when I joined them they had raised the referee to his feet but he looked very unsteady and was clearly in pain. He hobbled on in obvious distress but after half an hour he stopped running and called me over. It only took him a moment to decide that he should take my flag and I would replace him in the middle.

So, in the space of a few seconds in the rarest of circumstances, I found myself refereeing the cream of the cream of football, although it was of course in the most unfortunate circumstances for Mr Law and naturally I had great sympathy for him. Not only that, but later I would discover one of the most influential men in English football in its entire history was watching what I did. Anyway, there in the middle of players that would fetch heaven knows how many millions nowadays was me.

I really didn't have time to reflect, as I do now, that Ralph Tarratt, ex-farmer, ex-dentist's assistant, ex-insurance salesman, ex-grocer and ex-amateur footballer, a son of Horsham was now refereeing two of the finest teams playing in the First Division of the English Football League. My dad Ernest was sitting up in the stands watching the game and the world was truly at my feet. It was just as well then that my Acme Thunderer whistle had been prepared as meticulously as always.

I always put the whistle in boiling water before a game. No, not to clean it, but to get the sound right. That's what they told us to do, and it seemed to work. I always used the Thunderer right through my career, although to be honest the less I blew it the happier I was because it kept the game flowing for the crowd and the players.

The Acme Thunder has an interesting history. Hard-up toolmaker Joseph Hudson was for reasons yet undiscovered passionate about whistles in the 1860s and he set about making one for the Metropolitan Police. Legend has it that he got the right pitch when he accidentally dropped a violin. The Thunderer has been made since 1884 and long after I stopped using it in games is claimed to be the world's leading pea whistle. I am told that the firm makes 67 types of whistle, some of them without peas. They are used in orchestras, rescue work in tornados, life saving at sea, imitating crows, rooks, and ducks, and used by police forces throughout the world. I wonder how many of them know about my little boiling tip from 50 years ago.

Anyway my whistle seemed to be on perfect pitch for that Arsenal match as I gave up my linesman flag and re-started the game after taking over as referee from Mr Law, feeling nervous but confident that I could handle this important occasion. After a few minutes it seemed obvious that poor Mr. Law was limping heavily and could not be expected to run the line, so no sooner had we started than I had to stop the game for a second time. I went over to one of the Arsenal administrative staff and asked for a message to be put out over the public address system asking any League registered referee to come forward. Luckily there was an Essex League man in the crowd who agreed to take on the job of emergency linesman and the game could be re-started.

Within seconds the score was 2-0 with United's gifted inside-forward Stan Pearson scrambling the ball home after the Arsenal goalkeeper George Swindin dropped a cross at the United man's feet. Swindin had been a great Arsenal servant, winning three league title medals and an FA Cup winner's medal since signing in 1936 and he went on to play 299 times for Arsenal. The fans were clearly in the mood to lay the blame on someone else other than their Arsenal favourite and must have thought Swindin had been fouled, so they blamed me instead.

If I had any hopes for a quiet beginning to my career in top-class football they were about to be firmly squashed. Arsenal captain Joe Mercer led the protests from the players, and on the terraces the noisy North London home crowd were baying for my blood. Mercer, whose crooked-looking legs belied the absolutely wonderful football he could play, was a big figure in football then and would later manage England for six matches in 1974. He had already won a league title with Everton in 1939 playing with the legendary scorer Dixie Dean. Although it was thought the war had stolen his best years he proved a great servant to Arsenal, playing for them from 1946 until he broke a leg in 1954, playing five times for England and receiving an OBE for services to the game in 1976, 14 years before his death on his 76th birthday.

But on this day, mighty Mercer or not, I had given a goal before this huge crowd and I certainly did not intend to give way to mob rule. I called the Arsenal skipper over and told him that neither he nor his players would intimidate me and he should get on with the match. To his credit Mercer, whose name now lives on as one of football's gentlemen, just said to me: "Yes referee," and play re-started.

In a game like this it didn't take long for another decision by me to get the Arsenal fans and players hot under the collar again. Arsenal took the ball deep into the Manchester half on a surging run, the ball was crossed, heads clashed, and the crowd roared. "Penalty!" The Arsenal players pointed furiously to Henry Cockburn, the tough but talented 5ft 5ins ten stone United and England half-back, accusing him of 'hands'. Certainly the ball had been handled but I had clearly seen an Arsenal player control the ball with his hand and so I called for a free kick to United.

No one should think that football in the 1950s was played in a polite "Well done, chaps" atmosphere. People sought escape in huge numbers from the dull and dreary post-war everyday slog at football matches and they sometimes got hostile both with players and officials if their dreams were not delivered, as they still do now of course. I could almost feel the heat from the seething home fans.

In such a situation as a referee you feel exposed and the adrenaline rushes, but you are concentrating on trying to think clearly. In some ways, but not all, it's not unlike being a player, who has split seconds to make decisions that affect the course of the game and if you get it wrong you get in the neck from the crowd. This certainly, at any rate, was not the same in terms of atmosphere as refereeing a match in the Horsham League in front of three men and a dog on a rough farmland pitch as I had started in the early 1930s. No, I was truly playing with the big boys now.

The game continued to be fast and fierce and I could swear there was a black cloud hovering over the Arsenal supporters. If looks can really kill, I ought to have been six feet beneath the North London turf at that moment. Half time came. I walked with the linesmen towards the corner leading to our dressing room, with the boos and insults ringing in my ears from the dripping stands and a confetti of orange peel raining down upon my head.

"So this is it," I thought. But thinking back over the years, I can truly say that I had no fear for myself that day. That would come two years later, thousands of miles across the world in a much hotter atmosphere. No, at this moment at Highbury, I relished the opportunity I had been given and I could hardly wait for the second half to begin. When the players came back on the pitch I could see from the grim looks on the faces of the Arsenal players that they had been given quite a stiff dressing-down from their manager Tom Whittaker and they were determined to get back into the match.

Play went from end to end with both goalkeepers making fine saves but Manchester were clearly in command and when they scored their third goal through a Daniel own goal the result looked inevitable. Jimmy Logie, regarded as one of Arsenal's greats to this day, scored a late consolation goal for the

Arsenal but that certainly didn't satisfy the home crowd and when I blew the whistle to end the game they made their views on the parentage of the referee pretty clear. As I walked the gauntlet of rich abuse back to our changing room I heard myself described in all sorts of unrepeatable language, but despite that I still remember how happy I felt in knowing I had come through the match without any real problems.

As I sank into a deep hot bath I thought back over the game and felt quietly satisfied on a job well done. In those days Highbury, as now I suppose, offered superb facilities to match officials. As I lay in the enormous marble bath my boots were whisked away to be cleaned and a masseur waited to give me a rub down. But before I could take advantage of his services one of the linesmen called over to say that I was wanted at the door to our dressing room.

I was puzzled. Could there be a problem? As I climbed from the bath a tall, elegant man stepped through the door. It was Stanley Rous, the secretary of the Football Association from 1934 to 1961, president of FIFA from 1961 to 1974, the greatest referee of his day, one of the most senior men in the game and later knighted for his immense contribution. He also introduced the innovative diagonal system of "patrolling" a pitch used by thousands of referees in the past few decades.

"Just wanted a quick word Tarratt," said the tall, imposing Mr Rous. "I'm here with Mr Lester and we both thought you handled a difficult game very well. I'll be in touch." And he disappeared just as smoothly as he had arrived. I dropped onto the nearest bench. The Mr Lester that Mr Rous had mentioned was the FA's chief referee and if he and Stanley Rous were happy with my performance I really did have a lot to celebrate.

I had someone close by to share in my happiness. My dad, a staunch and loyal fan of Trinity, our local Horsham team where I had played for several years, had deserted his usual post by their halfway line and was in the stands here at

Highbury. I quickly dressed, said goodbye and thanks to the linesmen. What a day it had been, too, for the Essex League man who had turned up to watch and finished up running the line. I headed off to find dad. When I got to the spot where we had agreed to meet he was not there, but I did find an Arsenal steward waiting with a message for me.

The steward told me where Dad was – in the Arsenal boardroom having a cup of coffee. Two match tickets had been given for dad and that is how he ended up there. I was proud to have him sharing my big day and what a day it was. I don't know even now if the Arsenal fans ever forgave me, because, to make matters worse for them, United did the double on Arsenal that season, beating them 6-1 in their last league match to wrap up the title, their first since 1911. That day in North London I had leapt from a young lad's dreams to the real world of the English Division.

Some time after that memorable Highbury match I was presented with an orange at a referees meeting in Horsham. Showing a good sense of humour, my local colleagues had remembered that an irate Arsenal fan had lobbed one in my direction as I had left the pitch after that controversial match with United. Trying to be cool, I told the press when they picked up the story: "It was a bad shot. I didn't even have to duck."

Reporters at the Arsenal match noted the aggressive behaviour of the Arsenal team against me, who they obviously regarded as a "rookie" although I already had good experience of matches and had indeed refereed many Arsenal reserve matches or lined in their Division One games. Among the reports the Islington Gazette noted: "Some players apparently thought the deputy referee could be brow beaten and we had the unpleasant sight of players bickering at the official. But Ralph Tarratt, an experienced referee, stood firm."

J.T. Bolton in the Empire News of 9 December 1951 wrote: "Some players were inclined to take advantage of the deputy referee, but they got nowhere." Mr

Bolton also reported that my first task after taking over the whistle was to award United a goal when "Pearson hustled Swindin and ball over the line". That was his view of it from the press box, anyway. Bickering at referees? That makes me think now, what is it the French say? Something like 'the more things change the more they stay the same'?

Things were not always so grim between Arsenal fans and me. At senior level I had refereed Arsenal in October 1951 when they had better fortunes, winning 3-1 at Charlton, in front of a massive 69,500 crowd. It was a fantastically exciting match played in a memorable atmosphere with an under-strength Arsenal team falling a goal behind to Evans before Arsenal really turned it on, and two goals by Holton and one by Milton won it for them.

My old pal Sam Bartram had plenty to keep his hands warm in the Charlton goal, especially in the second half. It was a much less controversial affair than Highbury but thrilling to be refereeing in front of the huge crowd, filling the Valley's vast open terraces and loving the great football they were watching that day. The steep imposing banks of spectators reminded me that the Valley was literally dug out by supporters about 100 years ago, an incredible feat.

Moving on, or rather back a little, from Arsenal and Manchester United, one of the great joys of refereeing top-flight matches was to play a minor, and I always hoped unobtrusive, part in football history. When I blew the whistle to start Portsmouth's home Division One match with Fulham in September 1950 the team from the old naval town was beginning a second remarkable season in a spell of top level success that to this day has never been bettered, although their promotion to the Premier League in 2003 as Division One Champions was a tremendous achievement for the team and the city.

On that day half a century ago, I incurred the wrath of most of the 32,000 Pompey crowd by ruling out a goal by Pompey's Doug Reid because his team-mate Jimmy Froggatt was offside. The calls from the crowd in my direction were as salty as you might expect from such a sea-faring city crowd. It certainly was not as charming as the sound of the crowd singing that very distinctive and unique bell chime chant "Play up Pompey. Pompey play up" that survives to this day.

I always thought Pompey were a solid team with no great stars but plenty of excellent players driven on by their fine half-backs, especially the tough tackling dynamo Jimmy Scoular. Pompey won 1-0 and went on to overtake early rivals Newcastle and Manchester United to win the league for the second year running, a tremendous achievement, so my name was not mud with their fans for too long.

What a finish that season was. On the last day Pompey led on goal average, which they used in those days, from Wolves, and Sunderland, who were a point behind. All three had belting wins, and the telephone lines must have been buzzing when Wolves won 6-1, but Pompey's 5-1 impressive win over Aston Villa won the title. Some of the press had called Pompey unfashionable when they won the league in 48-49 but they were a good enough team unit to finish five points clear of Manchester United in the days when you got two points for a win.

That day at Fratton Park it was an honour to share the turf with two of the most loyal and consistent footballers in the history of the game. Crafty left-half and skipper Jimmy Dickinson would play an incredible 764 games between 1946 and 1965 for Pompey, and outside-right Peter Harris, who had a fair turn of speed, an impressive 479 times between 1946 and 1959. It would be silly to think nowadays that players back in those days did not think of bettering themselves and earning bigger pay packets by moving clubs.

But there was not quite so much greed (there was a maximum wage of £20 for ages) and not as much media rubbish surrounding the game then, and players could not make the massive amounts they do nowadays at the top level, both in their slice of transfer fees or wages. I think they got about a quid signing on fee in early post-war football and it did not matter whether they were sold for a fiver or £5,000.

I suppose even with a 10 per cent slice the top players could get £500,000 to a million pounds now just for changing clubs. Good luck to them, I say, if they can get someone to pay them these daft amounts, but my life as businessman making every penny work makes me think that someone will pay for it in the end. Dickinson and Harris seemed to me men who appreciated what they had, and looked after themselves so they could play as long as possible, and they gave Portsmouth unrivalled service not only in the glory years but in times when Portsmouth struggled.

Jimmy Scoular was as tough as teak. He was probably the dirtiest player in the Football League, although he was clever. I never got on well with Portsmouth at all. I thought of the top teams they were the dirty boys. They were so rough. I think referees had to be very strict with them. They were a good side, but a robust side.

I once crossed swords with the Pompey player Jimmy Froggatt but it was well away from any football pitch. Froggatt retired and took a pub at Partridge Green in Sussex, called The Green Man, and I got involved putting a Tarratt bar billiards table in there. I walked in one day because I heard there was a new landlord and I didn't know who he was. Jimmy saw me coming and said: "You again. Where have you popped up from?" So I said I'd come to talk about the table.

Jimmy said: "You can take the bloody thing away. I'll get my own." He didn't like me. He'd seen my name on the table you see. I was a dirty name for him. Jimmy had a very good bar billiards team there and our little confrontation had an interesting follow-up when his team staged a sort of mutiny over my table. Within a fortnight Jimmy said to me: "I have bought another table, but they won't play on mine, they have moved to the pub up the road." That gave me a chuckle.

But like me or not, Froggatt was a top player. So was Dickinson. He was a very nice fellow actually. He was a super guy. He stayed with them a long time, and he was a great servant to Pompey. He was no trouble on the pitch whenever I came across him.

There was a manager at Pompey who always hated me. He wore these bloody white spats and was a short-arsed little fellow, very plump, called Jack Tinn, who took them to a shock Cup Final win against Wolves in 1939. We never hit it off, and to this day I don't know why. "You again" the terse Tinn would say grimly as I walked into the ground. One day I had two guests with me, we were allowed guests, and he said: "You can have two tickets but you will not be allowed in the boardroom." Most clubs invited me in, but he would not let me in there.

The only time I ever got in the boardroom was when I met Monty (Viscount Montgomery, Portsmouth president), who I also met in Cairo during my war service. I took young Mick, one of the sons of my second wife, Edith, to many top games and he still vividly remembers the overwhelming excitement and passion of the atmosphere at Portsmouth. Mick told Phil Dennett during his research for the book: "Jimmy Scoular was at right half. His rule was that a player wasn't going to go by him with the ball. He would have him. Portsmouth were a bit of a dirty side then.

"I will always remember the fantastic way the crowd sang the Pompey Chimes. The first row would sway to the left and the second row would sway to the right. The third row would sway to the left and so on and while they were doing this they would all sing Play Up Pompey. It was something wonderful to see and to listen to. They were great days, going to games with Ralph. He'd take me to places like Arsenal and West Ham.

"I remember at a West Ham game when we came out of the ground they were selling papers that said Horsham had taken the lead in the FA Cup after 90 seconds against Notts County. There was great excitement, but they lost 9-1. Notts County had Tommy Lawton, so Horsham were up against it. When in another game he sent off Ronnie Rooke, the Crystal Palace player-manager, which caused a bit of a sensation, we got home and the neighbour said to him that some bloomin' ref had sent off Ronnie Rooke. Dad said to him all matter of fact: 'That was me'."

It was not just in Division One games that I brushed with great names. Even in lower league games I would come across men who would become legends lasting until the day you read this book. Every football fan worth his salt should know that Alf Ramsey managed the England team that won the World Cup for the first and so far only time in 1966. When I first came across him he was playing a steady and pretty cultured game for Tottenham in a Division 2 match at Luton on 22 October 1949.

Tottenham were top of the table and such was their reputation under Arthur Rowe for their fantastic, simple but exciting "push and run" style that the game drew a record ground attendance of 27, 319. Rowe liked players to control the ball, pass it quickly, and move into space for a return. It wasn't especially elaborate, but it was fast and wonderful to watch at its best, which was most times for a few seasons for that Tottenham side.

Ramsey was brilliant in his way. He was very cool player, calculating, and he seemed to be running the game through a computer in his head long before the things were much thought of. Polished maybe, but not quite a diamond to me because he rarely sparkled, just went about his job on the pitch with great professionalism. As a manager he was another one, just like Jack Tinn, who was not always very polite. He wasn't a popular man at all. He was all right with players though, they seemed to respect him and that 1966 World Cup winning team certainly played their heart out for him.

Alongside Ramsey that day I was refereeing at Luton was a busy player called Bill Nicholson, who was, like Ramsey, pretty withdrawn with the media and I got the impression he thought that talking about the game was a waste of time and it was what spectators saw happening on the pitch that mattered. God knows what he'd think now, with so much "tosh" being written and talked every day.

In theory, Nicholson has the best striking record of all England players, but I admit it is stretching a point a bit. He scored after only 29 seconds of his England debut when we beat Portugal 5-2 in 1951 at Goodison Park, but never played again, giving him a 100 per cent scoring record. He was chosen for the next match but cried off with injury. Interestingly enough in this age of club versus country selection rows he insisted that his fitness for Spurs took priority because, as he said at the time: "They pay my wages."

To me, Nicholson looked a tough, rather dour player but, as any real Spurs fan should know, he created the magical 1961 Spurs team. I found it hard to believe that Nicholson would go on to fashion such a dazzling team that was deservedly the first to win the League and FA Cup double then retained the Cup and went on to win a load more trophies including Tottenham's first EUFA cup win in 1972. But when I think back to that early champion Spurs side of 1949-50 and 50-51 I think Nicholson shrewdly adapted that direct "push and run style" for a more modern game a decade later.

I think that the 1960s Spurs side was one of the best British sides ever seen. Sadly I think from what I read over the years that Bill Nicholson was a little disillusioned with the attitudes of "modern players" when he quit the game many years ago. He was a very steady player, always good, never seemed to have a bad game when I saw him. He was not tremendously exciting but the 1961 side he produced was truly inspirational in the style of the football it played. He served Spurs loyally for his football lifetime and had a truly bizarre first match as Spurs manager in 1958 when they thrashed Everton 10-4 in front of a disbelieving White Hart Lane crowd.

No wonder then with those brains behind them in the 49-50 season when I came across them Spurs won the Division 2 title and then produced the remarkable feat of winning the Division One title at the first attempt after promotion. That afternoon Ramsey and Nicholson were just two good footballers doing the job they were paid for and I do not recall having one second of problems with them on the day. It was impossible to imagine what tremendous achievements lay ahead both for them and Tottenham.

Sometimes in the hurly-burly of a game I would see a youngster I just knew would make the grade at the highest level, even if he was playing at the time in a small-time match in front of a few thousand people and I was getting only brief glimpses of him because I had to concentrate on the job in hand. One of the finest young players I ever set eyes upon at close quarters was a 19-year-old called John Charles.

In November 1950 this giant 6ft 2ins of a young man, then registered with Leeds, turned out for an Army team against an FA team and I was the man in the middle at Highbury. He was described in at least one press report as trooper Charles. To my eyes, the lad was certainly built like a tank with huge powerful thighs but he also had a splendid touch on the ball, could cover ground very quickly, and was almost unbeatable in the air. Young as he was, Charles so inspired the unfancied Army team that they lost only 3-2.

Charles, of course, had already become at 18 the youngest centre-half to make his debut for Wales in March of that year in a 0-0 draw against Northern Ireland. He went on to become one of football's most versatile players and was equally powerful at centre-half and centre-forward, even playing at the top level in Italy for Juventus where he was adored. The 7,000 crowd and myself certainly got a glimpse of a genuine football talent that day and no matter what centre-half you might be admiring today he will not be better than Charles. He was a referee's dream, of course, never being sent off or even cautioned in a long career and I think the Italians called him the gentle giant.

As I began to climb the ladder as a referee football was riding on the crest of a post-war wave of popularity. In the 1948-9 season a record 41 million people had watched league football and for many years afterwards the game attracted huge crowds. I was forever reading in the newspapers of this record or that record being broken for crowds. It is unfair to compare crowd sizes then and now because society has changed so much with so many more distractions in the 21st century.

There was no saturation coverage 50 years ago on television, radio, and newspapers like today. If you really wanted to know how a game went, it was better to go to the match because there was no such thing as Match of the Day. All the same, it was interesting for me to compare crowds when I was looking at the attendance for a recent Second Division match. In April 2003 Wigan, who were at the time 12 points clear at the top, drew 7, 204 fans, in fact a decent crowd nowadays for them, for a 2-0 win at home to Brentford.

The equivalent division when I was refereeing was the Third Division, then split into North and South. I refereed one match at Millwall on 25 August 1951 when Brighton and Hove Albion beat them 3-0 and that drew a crowd of 26,583, about four times the Wigan gate. Although one reporter wrote about that Millwall game: "play became a little too robust at times" this must have been relatively trouble-free match between usually bitter "local" rivals because I was also quoted as saying it was "a pleasant match to handle."

Whilst I am on the subject of this match older Albion fans might remember that this team contained several of the best players ever to wear Albion's colours, so it was hardly a shock that they played some excellent football that day and indeed gave Albion one of the most convincing away wins against the Lions ever seen by Albion fans to this day.

Goalkeeper Jack Ball played one of his finest ever games for the Albion and made several superb saves. Looking back just before that great match, Ball had a most strange introduction to Albion, even for the late 40s when clubs tried all sorts of tricks to find a good side after the disruption of the war.

When Jack had made his debut at 18 a few years earlier they shifted the regular keeper Gordon Mee to the left wing to create room for him, surely something we would never see in modern-day football.

If that seemed strange the next game brought even more of a shock. Goalkeeper Ball found himself on the wing, although thankfully for him he later settled between the posts to play more than 160 times. Such strange shuffling of players did happen in the immediate post-war years, and perhaps they were a bit of a hangover from wartime games where clubs often struggled to field a side, frequently borrowing from other teams. By the 50s things were a good deal more organised and Brighton were certainly a solid and determined unit that day at Millwall.

In their ranks and busy firing them up with his enthusiasm in that match, as he did in so many others, was left-half Glen Wilson, a true Albion legend and a player of amazing stamina and tenacity, who later skippered them to their first-ever promotion to the Second Division in 1958. Wilson had two spells with the club as player and in other capacities between 1948 and 1986 season, appearing 436 times and many fans thought the off-handed manner of his dismissal from the back-room staff in 1986 was poor recognition of his hard work for the club.

Schemer Johnny McNichol, who from the glimpses I caught, pulled all the strings for Albion in that Millwall match, is still regarded as one of Albion's all-time finest players and it was no surprise to me when he was bought by Chelsea after making 165 Albion appearances between 1948 and 1952. It must have sickened the Albion fans though, but money talked in the game then, as it does even more now, and Albion were not well off by any means. McNichol cost Albion £5,000 from Newcastle and they got £12,000 got him, plus Chelsea's Jimmy Leadbetter in exchange. Wiry Leadbetter did Albion good service until 1955 scoring 33 times in 115 games and went on to win a League Champions medal with Ipswich in the early 60s.

I was fortunate enough to later see McNichol play for Chelsea when I refereed their home match against Portsmouth in Division One in August 1952 and he looked like he had made the transition up the League without too much trouble. In fact, his talent and versatility was shown by a note in the programme praising his display after an enforced switch to right-back from inside-right at Old Trafford the previous week after defender Sid Tickridge became, as the programme noted, rather grandly I thought as a plain-speaking person, "hors de combat " against Manchester United.

Chelsea lost that day 2-0 and John was quoted in the programme given to me for the Pompey game as saying he never wanted to play full-back again. I would have thought it was a waste of his talents anyway. Getting back to the Albion, despite their magnificent display that day against Millwall and being tipped for honours, Albion fell back to fifth place at the end of that season, but watching their progress I thought it was still a creditable performance.

Those local derbies like Albion-Millwall brought out massive attendances that only made officiating at them more enjoyable. People of a younger generation nowadays think it was all beer and skittles after the celebrations of winning the war, but the economy was in bad shape because of the massive cost of the war effort. Women, and it was mostly women who looked after the meagre family provisions, still had to present ration books to get basics and this went on well past 1950.

For millions it was a time of boredom and drudgery, despite everyone's obvious relief that the war was over. So football matches were a sort of Saturday afternoon release from a pretty humdrum existence, especially for factory workers and miners. That is why the crowds flocked back to football.

There were some marvellous teams and of course there was the wonderful Manchester United-Blackpool FA Cup final of 1948 that United won by four goals to two, still regarded as one of the best ever played. Stanley Matthews, who had become the first Footballer of the Year, played well but still finished on the losing side and had to wait until 1953 to get his winner's medal in that dramatic 4-3 win against Bolton.

But you have to remember that after the war clubs were in a state of flux and some of the football was to put it mildly "patchy." It did not seem to stop the enthusiasm of supporters, especially when they played their "neighbours." Rivalry got pretty fierce especially if the two teams were within the same city and the language got pretty ripe if the huge crowds thought you had made a boob.

When I refereed the local derby between Bristol Rovers and Bristol City in January 1950 a crowd of 33, 697 turned out for what was, after all, a Division Three South Game. In contrast, in April 2003 I see looking at a newspaper cutting that Bristol City drew 12,000 for a Nationwide Division Three promotion-chasing match and they were no doubt quite pleased with that.

Another Division Three match I handled at Coventry in April 1950 when they beat relegation strugglers Plymouth 3-0 attracted a crowd of 20,882, so the attraction of even lower division football was strong. Incidentally in that Plymouth match I awarded Coventry a penalty in the first minute for pushing, which did not endear me to those loyal Plymouth fans that had travelled by coach and train from the West Country and some choice language in Devon brogue floated in my direction. Despite the dialect it was clear what they meant.

In those days car ownership was far less common and anyway cars were generally less reliable and the motorway system we have now did not exist. I often drove to games but fans generally took coach excursions or special trains were run, and very few fans actually drove to either home or away games.

Talking of Plymouth, I had made my debut as an FA Cup referee in their shock 1-1 third round draw with mighty Wolves a few months earlier in January 1950.

What a game for me to make such a debut. I recall there were about 40,000 there and Wolves, in their black and gold, had names like Johnny Hancocks, a nippy and wonderful footballer who wore only size five boots, and the dazzling winger Jimmy Mullen. And of course Wolves had the great centre half Billy Wright in their ranks, who went on to play a world record 70 consecutive matches for England.

Strangely, one memory I have of that game is little to do with refereeing. It was the sight of ill people or those recovering from operations watching in what looked like long wicker beds on wheels wheeled out in front of the vast crowd. No doubt the roars of the crowd provided some sort of tonic for them along with Plymouth's creditable result.

My local football connections had led me to getting a rather luxurious lift down to Plymouth for that wonderful Wolves tie. I used to referee a lot in Crawley. And I did a lot of friendlies for Crawley Football Club when they were at home, including one against Chelsea. Town Mead, where Crawley played until they moved to Broadfield Stadium, was usually a mud bath in those days, but then a lot of pitches were. They did not have the technology or the attention in those days.

I think games went on in far worse conditions than they do now. The pitches were not so well drained and lot of them were on clay anyway. Some matches were inches deep in mud, but we muddled through most of them OK otherwise we would never have got the leagues finished. Leaping ahead a bit to when I was helping run local football the heavy snow of 1961-62 did us in for weeks on end.

We were trying to get games on but it was hopeless. Teams were spending days trying to save matches and still finding the pitches were so bone hard they were lethal. You had to consider the safety of the players. In a way it was the same for professionals as amateurs. The "pros" risked ending their career and the park players risked losing their pay if they got crocked.

One unlucky injury in the normal course of a game was unfortunate but to add to the risks by playing on a potentially dangerous surface was not justified. Spectators sometimes thought it was great fun to see defenders slipping and sliding on icy pitches, but believe me I felt for the lads who were trying to be professional and play and at the same time save themselves from breaking something. Mud was bad, but apart from the odd slide, like that one at Highbury in '51 that had such dramatic consequences for me, it was not quite so dangerous.

You were more likely, and this applied to referees as well as players, to get pulled muscles where parts of the ground were glue pots and others were hard. Players would hare down the wing at full stretch, taking off from a firm patch of pitch and then put a foot in a soggy patch and that would be the end of their game. Even with their professional level of fitness, they suffered pulled muscles and tears, but the standards on grounds, and that includes a lot of council grounds that have been drained in the past 20 years or so, are now much better.

Returning to my association with Crawley and the FA Cup tie at Plymouth, Norman Longley C.B.E the builder, who became president of Crawley Football Club, was a mate of mine and when he heard I was refereeing Plymouth Argyle at Home Park in the third round of the FA Cup against mighty Wolves, he asked me for tickets. Of course I said yes, I had some spare, and after that I was taken down in his car, which was a Daimler, driven by his chauffeur, to the match.

It was done in style and we all had a great day and the match had a wonderful tense atmosphere with the Plymouth crowd thinking they might just topple Wolves, for whom Billy Wright was outstanding in helping them to a replay. I remember Lady Longley; she used to do all the weather reports for the Evening Argus. She had all her equipment down the bottom of her garden. She was a lovely lady. After that treat of a trip with Sir Norman in his Daimler I also did the replay. Wolves must have kept something up their sleeves, and showed their class, winning 3-0, and it was a thrill to officiate in front of 43,835 that day.

I got to know Billy Wright reasonably well and once I went out to dinner with him and the Beverley sisters, who were the first British girl group to make the Top Ten charts in the USA in 1956. When he married one of them, called Joy, it made world headlines. The other two, Teddie and Babs, were identical twins and they told me they were born on Joy's birthday. They had a cute hit called Sisters. They were really silly, giggly girls, and great fun to be with but they had their heads screwed on when it came to their careers. Billy seemed to me to be a very soft kind of man, although intelligent and no pushover, but he was not soft on the pitch. He was hard but skilful and I would put him in the top ten of post-war footballers that I saw.

I was amused after the Plymouth cup tie that a press report said that I "proved a very unbiased official". "I should hope so", I thought when I stuck that into my cuttings book. It seems a bit of a patronising comment now I am reminded of it looking at my cuttings, but I think at the time I was glad of the compliment, however back-handed it might appear now. I mean, what else would they expect me to be?

While on that point of "bias" it was a curious feature of football in those times that I was often chosen to referee Brighton and Hove Albion matches during my career, either at League or Combination level, despite the fact that I came from Horsham in Sussex and lived only about 20 miles from the Albion's Goldstone

Ground. It would not be allowed now, I suppose, although there was never any hint of problems with the exception of one Albion game that I shall relate later.

I still did plenty of local football, and living in Horsham did not prevent me from being appointed to one of Horsham Football Club's biggest home wins in their history, when they thrashed Old Malvernians 11-1. I cannot recall why the visitors were so bad, but nothing I or anyone else could have done could have saved them that day. Horsham were on their top form and the visitors were out of their depth. I never felt sorry or glad for any teams I refereed, I couldn't afford to, but it seemed to me a thrashing like the one Horsham dished out was actually little fun for Horsham after the fifth or sixth goal and was of course misery for Malvernians. Most players would probably agree with me, I think. They like a challenge.

Looking back at some old programmes it was not difficult to see why Horsham gave teams a good hiding more than 60 years ago because they were so strong. When Kent played Sussex at Canterbury in February 1937, when I was on the line, six of the eleven were Horsham players, including Jack Broadley who was a quite an outstanding outside-right and probably one of the best ever to play for the club.

Although I have not seen the modern team, if there has been better than the old Horsham team, they would have to be pretty special. For the record, since I have the programme in front of me, Hornets history fans might be interested to know the mighty Horsham players that day against Kent were Ragless and Mayer at full-backs, Cope at left-half, and Broadley, Hewitt, and Browning as forwards. That crowd was pretty docile at Canterbury for that match, but someone wasn't prepared many years later to give me the benefit of the doubt when Albion played Aldershot in February 1949 and I gave a penalty to Brighton late in the game, which finished 1-1.

Not even the fact that the Shots young goalkeeper Ron Reynolds saved it could cool one idiot down in the 8,000 crowd. The Daily Express reported my complaint that I had been hit on the way down the players tunnel, I don't remember the details now, but it showed even before I reached First Division matches how worked up some of the "daffier" members of a crowd could be. Later in the book I will tell you just how heated things could get, including the most frightening match I ever handled, but in the next chapter I want to tell you about another very important part of my life which survives and indeed thrives to this day.

2   BAR BILLIARDS SWEEPS SUSSEX

Hand in hand with all this refereeing, I had to make a living and starting the Tarratt bar billiards table business was the biggest part of my business life.

Hundreds of pubs still have tables with the name Tarratt on them and I am very proud of that side of my life, which is now run by my son Rod. The start of my bar billiards business was an indirect result of my quest to keep fit for my refereeing after injury stopped me from playing football in my early twenties. A football referee has to be in good shape if he is to be able to keep up with the play and in all my experience the best referees are the ones who are up to speed with the play right through the game.

So keeping match fit was a way of life for me and over the years I trained in many different places and had many training partners. In 1930 I often trained alongside Gordon Clayton, an optician who had a shop in Park Street, and he was also a keen member of Horsham Rugby Club. One day he asked me if I had any thoughts of moving on from the grocery shop that my young wife Billie and I ran at Park Street, Horsham.

Billie was small, petite I suppose you would say, she was a pretty and lively girl, and I was very attracted to her. By the time we married in May 1936 our child Sonia was already on the way and she came into the world in a private nursing home, which was later taken over by soldiers in the war, on 2 December. I was already thinking of new ways to help the finances of the family.

Never being one to turn an idea down without giving it some thought, I asked Mr Clayton what he had in mind. It seemed he had a pal, a Mr Sherlock who raised chickens over Billingshurst way and he was looking for a man to manage a new game that was about to be launched in Great Britain.

Called 'bar billiards' it appeared to be the ideal game for pubs and clubs because, from the landlord's point-of-view, it was a good money-spinner, thanks to the unique time clocks which determined the exact length of time that a game would last. Therefore, unlike darts, crib, or any other pub game of the time, the players would have to pay for every new game that they played.

I learned that the special time clocks were patented by a French firm and so could not be copied and that a London company, Jelkes in the Holloway Road, was to make the tables. I would be responsible for negotiating sites, installing them, maintaining them and collecting the money. The man behind the idea was a gentleman farmer, and he had the exclusive rights to site the tables in my local area, retaining a percentage of the taking for his trouble.

At that time the price of playing a game was 6d. That was for 20 minutes of playing time. Well, it did not take me long to decide that this was just up my street. Through my football contacts I knew a fair few landlords and club managers and I realised that by joining the Licensed Victuallers Association I would be able to meet many more. Billie kept on the shop and I worked in the business, which I later called 'Sussex Bar Billiards'.

The first table I sited was at the 'Wheatsheaf' pub in Cuckfield and they had a great success with that. Word spread within the trade and in no time we were inundated with orders. Like any new business it took a little time to find our feet but once Jelkes began to step up production we never looked back and we never seemed to stop to catch our breath because we were so busy dealing with new customers.

I well remember early in the operation, on a bright Sunday morning, I got my dad out of bed early to help me load a table onto the farm trailer I used to tow behind my old car, an elderly Austin 7. With dad alongside we set off over the Downs for the 'Eagle' in Brighton but when we jumped out of the car in the pub car park we found the trailer was empty. Panic set in. We re-traced our route and at the foot of a very steep hill we found three policemen puzzling over a strangely shaped table covered in green baize that might have dropped from the skies, there being no indication of its origins. When they realised that our trailer had neither sides nor a tailgate they were less than amused but in the end we got away with a caution – just.

All the indications were that bar billiards was going to be big business for me. Orders for more tables were coming in thick and fast and clearly the public were taking the game to their hearts. Soon the pubs and clubs were forming teams and, just like darts, leagues were an obvious development. My next step then was to set up my first league and I chose to stay close to home and establish the first in Horsham.

We soon followed it with leagues in Mid Sussex, Eastbourne, Littlehampton, Billingshurst, Worthing, Lewes, Hastings, Crawley and Brighton, where there were four divisions. Soon the area contained more than 500 tables making up some 14 bar billiard leagues by the mid-1930s. Later I established the Sussex County Association with a County Finals competition and from there we extended the competition out into Kent, Surrey, and Hampshire, forming the Southern Counties Association.

This was an exciting time for me. The orders came in for more and more tables and it was all I could do to keep up with demand, while at the same time my refereeing career was beginning to take off. I had risen through the ranks from being a Class 1 referee in the Sussex County League to being nominated for the Football Combination list. As that was happening Charlie Webb, who had been the Brighton manager since 1919 and was something of a legend in the club, had put me forward to the Southern League, and it gave me a great opportunity to widen my experience.

Promotion to the Linesmen's List soon followed and then I was added to the Supplementary List, which meant I could take on Football League Third

Division games. Soon I reached the top of the ladder and was appointed to the full Football Association Referees List in 1948. Now I was eligible to referee at the highest level. It had been a long journey and one that needed a fair amount of luck but I had achieved an ambition that had looked a very long way off when I first took a whistle onto the pitch. At the same time the bar billiards business was set for expansion and it continued to grow over the years.

Later in life, after I suffered the loss of my second wife Edith to cancer, I was lucky enough to meet the woman who would not only become my third wife but also help me run the business and play a large part in it. I first met Joy at the Foresters in Kirdford, where she was working behind the bar.

At the same time a large firm in Ascot and some good friends of mine had organised a bar billiards competition set-up with possibly even more teams involved.

Ken Hussey was the manager of Bar Billiards Ltd and he became Secretary of the All England Association. He also was the instructor of the annual match with the Channel Islands, who played home and away. It was an event greatly looked forward to and usually our party consisted of at least 200. We even managed to win, but they had some good players.

In August 1978, when I was then the Chairman of the All England Bar Billiards Association I managed to persuade Reginald Bosanquet, the newscaster, to be our first President. I became friendly with him when he wanted a table for his London flat and when he moved down to Rudgwick we used to meet at the Oakwood Hill Inn where they had one of our tables, and I certainly had to watch the drinking side of things.

I remember at one of his parties drinking his famous old port, and I was out of action for a couple of days after that session. Possibly my best memory of him was at one of our finals nights held at the Sun Alliance Club when he presented our trophies. His chauffeur, who was in the car with Reggie and his current girlfriend, said that Reggie was in a hopeless state – yet he walked onto the stage looking as if he hadn't had a drink for years.

Reggie presented the trophies, thanked the audience, and stayed for an hour, and he had come straight from reading the nine o'clock news. He was a great help to me in setting up the first TV coverage of our game. It was a programme Yorkshire Television put out on a Tuesday lunchtime, with Freddie Truman, famous of course for his fast bowling with England and Yorkshire, (he took 307 wickets for an average 21.57) and his witty after-dinner speaking, as the commentator.

Quite a number of our league players won places including my son, Rod, who got through to the quarter-finals. After Reggie died Bill Maynard became our president. We later decided to purchase our tables from a firm based in Hoddesdon, Sams Brothers, and also put up the price of playing to one shilling. When this firm eventually switched to producing golf equipment we "pinched" one of their best men to join us as our general manager. His name was Dennis Brisley, and he was a great asset to us in the build-up of the business.

It was during this period that I decided to expand and we started siting tables in the Doncaster area where I had an excellent manager, Charlie Wheeler. A man of repute in the bar billiards world, he soon set about forming a strong league that eventually joined the All England Association. By this time the price of play had risen to 50p and even the out of work miners were willing to pay this.

At this stage two large breweries decided to operate their own tables and set up their own teams to run it. This of course was a big blow, but in a little over 18 months they realised they were out of their depth and asked us to carry on where we had left off. However, it would be at a price that meant that our profit from the tables was definitely cut. It was not long before we realised we were in trouble.

The price of tables in clubs had risen sharply and as the venture to Yorkshire was over-stretching us with the very long distances between the works and the operation, I decided to pull out. It had been too adventurous. Even with this withdrawal things did not pick up, so I decided, against the advice of all the other operators, to double the price of play up to a £1. You can imagine the uproar, and a meeting was called.

There were angry protest letters in the press, but in a matter of weeks it was all accepted, and everything calmed down. All the other operators quickly followed suit, which proved I had been right in the first place. After things had settled down, Joy and myself decided to put the company on the market and Rex Williams, the snooker player who ran a company in Birmingham, made us an offer of £500, 000 but it meant us taking a lot of shares in his company.

Then to my surprise my son, Rod who was working for the company, asked if we would like to consider him taking over and we both agreed, and told Rex of our decision. A few weeks after the handover I picked up the newspaper. On the business page was a headline that the Williams company had gone into liquidation and its manager had been arrested. I thought what a lucky let off that was for us.

Rod has developed the firm in very difficult times, introducing pool and going into London. With the drink and driving laws and more pubs closing and specialising in food it hasn't been easy, but they weathered the storm by cutting costs. With satellite television of big football matches, pool and jukeboxes it is hard for pubs to keep up an interest in bar billiards now but there are still many leagues running, though now with fewer teams.

The economics of the game do not look so good however and I do not think bar billiards will stand many more price increases. All the same, it is pleasing to see leagues like the Mid Sussex Tarratt Pool League thriving so long after I first launched the game in the county. The Mid Sussex Times at Haywards Heath reported in 2003 that they were running a summer league that started in July 2003 so it is good to think the game is still popular in an age where there are so many counter-attractions. Maybe the simplicity of the game still appeals to people as things get more complicated, anyway I hope people continue to enjoy it because it has given me a lot of fun and of course helped me make a living.

In the first part of this book I told you about the big break I had with that 1951 Arsenal match, but it was a long climb up the League ladder to the First Division, as any Premier League referee would tell you now. After injury prematurely ended my own playing days short in my early 20s, I had cut my teeth in the 1930s refereeing in the local leagues, and things sometimes got a bit tough out there. It didn't help when first starting out to hear stories about how referees in the past had been ducked in ponds for giving "dodgy" decisions, although luckily I escaped that fate.

I quickly learned you did indeed need eyes in the back of your head. In one match at the Dripping Pan in Lewes, one of the best-known football grounds in Sussex, a Lewes supporter ran down an embankment and hit me behind the ear. But unluckily for him I was having none of it and he made the mistake of thinking he had got away with it as he fled into the crowd. But I was so annoyed that I ran after him and caught him.

Things got even blacker when I was knocked out after one of the Roffey Institute players smacked me across the mouth in a game and knocked me to the ground against Broadbridge Heath on 23 November 1935, the first time in recorded football history a referee at local level had been so badly assaulted. It was just after I had been promoted to handle Sussex County League matches. I'd only taken on the Roffey game to do the teams a favour after the appointed referee cried off at the last minute, and that was the thanks I got.

There was a lot of talk about cleaning the game up after this, but it was an isolated incident as far as I was concerned. As a result of the attack two Roffey players, Lesley Luxford and Leonard Penticost, got suspended for life and Roffey's ground was closed for a month, a pretty hefty and I must say totally justified decision.

The difference between parks games and top professional matches was that at a pro game there were police officers on duty at top games whereas there were none at parks games. If a couple of players really lost their cool you were entirely dependant on some of the other players calming them down, and on the rare occasions things got out of hand you could feel extremely vulnerable. Fortunately, the vast majority of local players played the game in the best spirit although the tackling, especially in those heavy round toecap boots with their nailed-in leather studs, made me shudder sometimes.

The two players in that notorious Roffey game, who pleaded guilty to assault at the petty sessions, as the courts were known then, also got find £1 each for assault and banned for life from attending matches. It all happened after I ordered another player off. As I noted the name, Penticost tried to hit me and Luxford rushed in and did manage to hit me. Needless to say, the game was abandoned with 14 minutes left and the press made much of it all.

The assault did make me feel a bit sick about things, and I did consider quitting the game after this violence. However, the local association asked me to reconsider. Fortunately I carried on and of course was lucky enough to have a good career. The football authorities backed me all the way in the criminal prosecution, because they wanted players to know they could not get away with that sort of thing. I should think it was of the first criminal prosecutions of its kind for a football offence.

I was never physically assaulted again, although there were occasions when I felt I was coming rather close to getting a thump from a player or someone in the crowd who was getting very hot under the collar with a decision they obviously did not agree with.

One thing I noted in the local football as I climbed the ladder was the big crowds that turned out for non-League football. There was still a good deal of enthusiastic support for smaller clubs, and people identified more then with local teams like Haywards Heath, Horsham, Worthing, and Lewes, where players more often than not were living in the area and known by everyone in the crowd. More than 3,000 turned out at Horsham when I took charge of the 1937 Sussex Senior Cup semi-final in which a good Haywards Heath side beat East Grinstead 3-0. In one match at Victoria Park in Haywards Heath, in about 1936 I think, a crowd of 1,000 people watched Hastings and St Leonards, then regarded as the "Arsenal of Sussex" thrash Haywards Heath 9-1, and about 500 of the gate travelled west from Hastings.

Nowadays I suppose Haywards Heath, former league champions but fallen on harder times and only promoted from Division Three of the County League in 2002-3, would be lucky to attract 100 fans to their large stadium at Hanbury Park, possibly still the most spacious in the county league. Incidentally, on the Hastings side that day was Harry Parks, the well-known cricketer, who had previously played for Heath, so that gave things an extra edge.

In another match at Victoria Park in November 1935 Haywards Heath had a bit more luck, beating Eastbourne Comrades 6-1. The Mid Sussex Times newspaper was fair enough to note: "Mr R E Tarratt refereed the game most efficiently." Even at senior Sussex County League level I found myself noting down some silly scores in my notebook. The ones I recall or noted especially were Worthing 13 Bexhill 1, and then Worthing topped that when they banged in another 13 against Bognor.

My local team Horsham beat Old Malvernians 11-1, and at the time were league champions. These mighty "hammerings" led to calls in the press to forget the constant chatter about starting a County League Division Two and improve the quality of the existing single division, but eventually over the next half a century a second division and then a third were started.

When I noted down eight goals for Haywards Heath against Hove's nil in April 1937 it took Heath's goal scoring for the season to a remarkable 99. I always seemed to be bumping into Heath in those days. On that day I noted centre forward Lyan scored five and the records showed he scored more than 30 that season, though I suppose he is just another long-forgotten local football star now.

In that same year higher up the football scale I came across the other, unglamorous, face of professional football, seeing players slogging somewhat anonymously in the reserves and hoping for a break into the first team. For some of the young players I saw there was always hope and they were full of energy and optimism, but some of the older ones were fighting injury and tired legs and were on the slippery slope to the end of their careers, usually with little or no money to show for it.

When I officiated in the Albion-Arsenal reserve match in 1937 two of Albion's finest goal scorers of all time were doing their time in the "stiffs", as the reserve team was rather unkindly called by supporters. Bert Stephens, although a winger, eventually set the astonishing record of scoring a goal every other match in the first team during his career with Albion from 1935 to 1948, making him the club's all-time most prolific scorer.

This was a truly incredible feat when you consider he often missed matches in wartime because of call-outs to his much more important fire duties. Modern fans might say he scored a lot of goals when football was a little disorganised in wartime competition, but his 174 goals from 366 games included 87 in the league before wartime competitions started so there is no doubting his pedigree.

His story of a career robbed of its peak by the war is not, sadly, that unusual, but you didn't hear players like him moaning about it. They knew some players fighting abroad had paid a much higher price. Albion's third-highest scorer at first team level of all time, the lively Scot Jock Davie, was alongside him on that day. About half Jock's 120 goals from 191 games between 1936 and 1946 were scored in wartime competitions but, as in the case of Stephens, that did not detract from his achievement. They looked a likely pair that day.

Davie also had the unusual distinction of playing for no less than 19 other teams during the war, when teams were often patched together to fulfil fixtures, and actually scored a hat-trick against Albion in 1941 when playing for Queens Park Rangers. These were indeed unusual times to be playing football but there was a grim determination to keep the game alive despite the carnage going on around the world.

Stan Risdon was in the Albion reserve side that day in 1937 against Arsenal, but he went on to captain the Albion for seven seasons and even turned out in goal. Although the war stole away his best years of top-level league football, like hundreds of other players, he played until 1948.

Albion's left-half on that day, Jack Dugnolle, had the distinction of being the only professional player in the UK born on the wild North West Frontier between Pakistan and Afghanistan, a place that seemed really distant and mysterious in those days. Hove-educated Jack had two spells with Albion before and after the war, but by the time he settled in the side his youthful promise had evaporated into the veteran stage of his career. He later joined the powerful Horsham team, winning a Metropolitan League medal with them in his first season in 1951, and later coached and managed Worthing.

As was often the case as clubs tried new players, some never enjoyed a good run in the first team. One of the promising lads in that reserve side was 21-year-old right-half Harry Brophy, a Surrey fast bowler, who played only one first team game for Albion from 1936-38 despite having been an outstanding schoolboy player and on the professional books of mighty Arsenal at only 17.

Harry broke a leg in 1936, although he did recover to play nearly 40 Second Division games for Southampton before war broke out.

While handling all these matches and indeed right through my career I was also keen enough to learn from my own mistakes and from watching others. And I have always believed that the referee should never be the star of the show, although nowadays there is tendency to pick referees to pieces with television cameras and endless re-runs of incidents.

My fascination with refereeing extended to my cuttings books where I kept clippings of famous referees like Harry "Natty" Nattras, GT Gould and WP Harper, amongst many. At the same time I met first class people like George Cook, a manager at Shiphams in Chichester, and my lifelong pal Peter Wilkins, who would have made top class referees under different circumstances, so the best didn't always make it to the top, much to my disappointment.

As I made progress as a referee I was becoming something of a local celebrity on the football front. I suspect I may have added to my notoriety when I was handling one particular match, a 3rd round tie in the FA Amateur Cup, the date of which I cannot recall or trace. A truly horrible tackle was committed by one of the Corinthian Casuals and I had no hesitation in whistling up the offending player. The Casuals, of course, were supposed to be renowned for their sporting amateur attitude.

This did not stop them having enough steel about them to reach the Amateur Cup Final in 1956, losing only after a replay to Bishop Auckland. This particular Casuals player was indignant as I reached for my notebook. "Just a moment referee," he said, glaring into my face. "You can't caution me. Don't you know who I am?" I said: "Certainly I do Mr. Swanton," as I wrote his name down in my black book, "and it makes no difference to me." Uttering an exceptionally rude word, particularly for a Corinthian, a team renowned for their good manners on the field of play, the celebrated newspaper columnist and later radio cricket commentator E.W. Swanton turned his back and the game continued.

At this point, as a follower of the Albion's history, I think it is of interest to note that back in 1922 Brighton and Hove Albion under Charlie Webb had played an important part of the Corinthians history, entertaining them before 23,000 people when they played in the FA Cup for the first time. Their charter had forbidden them to play anything but "friendlies" until then, although the side was at one time so good, with several internationals, it regularly thrashed League sides in what we might call today friendlies but which were money-spinning competitive matches for the Corinthian club, although not its players.

Refereeing one of their games, I could not help but sense their unique place in the history and spirit of the game, although they knew the commercial value of "friendly" matches against top professional teams. Their claims to fame include a "friendly" thrashing of a Manchester United side 11-3 in 1904 in a non-league but deadly serious match at Leyton that is still recorded as the biggest defeat in a first class match that United have suffered. The Times stated the obvious I suppose in saying: "In the second half Manchester United were quite outplayed"

This perhaps might not have been the shock it seems now, looking at the Corinthians astonishing wins against the so-called top-flight professional teams. Before meeting United, Corinthians had already defeated in similar matches the 1884 FA cup winning Blackburn side 8-1 and the 1903 winners Bury 10-3. And long before playing the Albion they had beaten Football League champions Aston Villa 2-1 in the Sheriff of London shield, which was their first attempt to win any trophy.

After that 1-1 draw in the historic first FA Cup match on 13 January 1923, which attracted national interest, it took Albion two replays to beat Corinthians, ending in a 1-0 win at neutral Stamford Bridge on a midweek afternoon on 22 January 1923 before an astonishing 43,000 crowd. Albion's young scorer

Tommy Cook, from Cuckfield, became an Albion legend, played for England, and unhappily had one of the briefest-ever spells of Albion management at seven months from May 1947. He also played cricket for Sussex.

From the available reports it seems that Brighton's "robust" tackling broke up the Corinthian's short sharp passing game and it appears the forward line of the amateurs was nowhere near as punchy as 20 years previously, although the defence was as good as Brighton's.

I hear now that Corinthians have not made quite such great progress, and are now in the Rymans League, where they finished in the bottom half of the Division One South in the 2002-3 season, whereas in my day they were proud members of strong Isthmian League whose clubs drew crowds that many Football League clubs would envy nowadays. But it is nice their name lives on, so long after my encounter with Mr Swanton.

As the end of the 1930s neared and Europe began to become menacingly unsettled by Nazi military ambitions the Football Association and the Football League were asked by the British government to come up with a scheme to keep the game going even though there were now travel restrictions preventing supporters getting across the country to away games.

The football authorities re-organised the leagues into regions and the scheme worked very well with teams playing their neighbours wherever possible.

Sadly though, however the radio and papers reported the news, we all knew that the war was not going well for our boys and I think we knew too that we were all in for a long haul. I well remember receiving a telegram and then a confirmation letter changing the kick-off time of the match between Arsenal and Sunderland on the 2 September 1939. The message, from Arsenal manager George Allison, told me that owing to the excavation of children from London out to the country transport problems would be eased by changing the start time to 5pm.

Only the day before I was due to take part in a referees quiz between teams from England and Scotland. It was due to be broadcast on the National Programme on the wireless, as radio sets were called in those dim and distant days. But the quiz was cancelled, said the message I received, "due to the impending war." I have vivid memories of those unsettling and increasingly tragic times, in particular the last match I was involved in before my own war was to begin.

It was at Selhurst Park on the outskirts of London and was a League game between Crystal Palace and Brighton. At the time air raids, or often merely the threat of them, had created turmoil in attendances because games were often shortened or even abandoned. I remember hearing in football circles that one match involving the Albion at Southampton on 21 September 1940, a game that I was fortunately not involved with, had been abandoned after only about three minutes, which was obviously a huge disappointment to fans and players. They managed only 45 minutes when they tried again in October and enemy aircraft flew over the ground.

As the war went on things got rather bizarre at times, with teams quite often setting out with only four or five players and hoping to patch together a full side when they got to the game. The story doing the rounds 63 years ago was about a farcical Albion match that perfectly illustrates the struggle the game had to survive during wartime.

The Albion set out on Christmas Eve for one Christmas Day match in 1940 at Norwich with not even half a team and borrowed some Norwich reserves, a Bolton centre-half, as well as a couple of soldiers from the 1,419 crowd. The farce was complete when they lost 18-0, but reading about it at the time you couldn't help admire the stubborn will to carry on. On the other hand lucky Aldershot, famed for its military barracks, at one time had the whole brilliant England half-back line turning out, Britton, Cullis, and Mercer because they happened to be stationed there. So at least someone occasionally got some benefit from all this war football chaos. Albion's lucky break was to have a good part of the Liverpool team stationed for a while in 1941 nearby, and Charlie Webb made good use of them as Albion hit a good run.

I had officiated on the line at a good many Albion matches and obviously being a Sussex lad had followed their fortunes. Only about six months earlier in 1940 Albion had lost 10-0 to Palace in front of a crowd of 7,500 but the Battle of Britain in August and subsequent enemy air activity had often made people reluctant to leave their homes for the exposed environment of football match in an open arena. Bear in mind that in those days there were no all seater stadiums and a good deal of the terracing was open to the skies.

On that particular day I was officiating at Selhurst Park, on 7 September 1940, long after the Albion thrashing, the Crystal Palace programme noted that the attendance at the previous home match had been "greatly affected by an air raid alarm" which led to many thousands staying at home on a sunny day. For the visit of Albion a friend gave me a lift to the gates and it was good to see that despite everything there was a decent crowd for wartime of about 1,500 streaming into the ground.

Before the game Charlie Webb, manager of Brighton, kindly offered me a ride back to Sussex in the team coach after the game that I was later glad to accept. We kicked off in what was more of a friendly than a league match. The roar of the crowd had at first partially drowned the drone of enemy 'planes coming over, the deep boom of exploding bombs and the thump of the anti-aircraft guns, but at half-time players and supporters alike could hear the sounds of war all too clearly.

Although we did not realise it at that moment, we were witnessing the start of the Blitz. Brighton lost five goals to two, but, although we officials and players concentrated professionally on the job in hand, it seemed everyone's mind was on other things and I knew that soon I would have to play my part in serving my country. One of Albion's goals that day was scored by outside-left Bert Stephens, who as I record elsewhere, was, game for game, one of Albion's most lethal marksman ever.

Taking up Charlie Webb's offer of a lift home to Sussex I got on the team bus, and it proved a sombre trip home for us all. The bus stopped at Croydon and we all stepped out to look at the glow of the fires burning in the distance in the City of London. I was later dropped off at home and the other lads were driven on to Brighton. The sight of those flames had shocked us all. It was a very sad end to the day and the memory of it lives with me still. Of course, we knew a war was on but I think this day we began to realise that it was very soon going to change our lives, if not take some of them, and it was a sobering ride home that day.

On a lighter note, during this period I later ended up having a cartoon strip in the Daily Mirror. I did not draw it of course but I did provide the footballing stories and the coaching tips for the illustrator and the cartoons appeared on six days each week. I cannot recall now how it all started.

Sadly, it was to be replaced before too long and the war played a part in that.

But we could not complain too much. After all our place was taken by the gorgeous 'Jane' who added a whole new meaning to cartoon strip and was certainly a tonic for the troops. Certainly the lads in the services did not seem to mind the change and 'Jane' quickly became the forces favourite. I was obviously no match for a bit of a glamour girl.

I think I knew that soon my time would cease to be my own and there would be others deciding how I would be spending my days. I had a family to consider of course. I was now the proud father of two daughters, Sonia who was born in 1936, soon after Billie and I married, and Wendy, who followed her in 1940. Then there was the bar billiards work to consider.

Billie was confident that she would be able to run both family and my bar billiards work on her own if I joined up, so there seemed to be nothing else to do but get ready to go and 'do my bit'. Sonia recalls how during the war she saw Billie checking all the index cards so she could make the calls on the pubs, and often heard the story of how Billie drove to Kent collecting rents under threat of the constant air raids and in blackout conditions.

As for me personally, our country was at war and I decided the time had come for me lend a hand and volunteer for the RAF. Yet I was to find in the next five years that my refereeing was to be in demand in the hottest theatres of war, and I would meet up with some friendly football faces from the days of the peacetime I had left behind.

3   WAITING TO GO TO WAR

The first thing that happened to me in wartime service was that my chances of survival improved by about 1000 per cent because I was not fit. Then a snooker table saved my life. After this I was given a job running a brothel. And I ended the war broken hearted at the most terrible news from my wife.

That was all yet to come as I rolled up at the Brighton recruiting station for the Royal Air Force, which was the place I chose to make my entry into the Second World War. The Allies were still falling backwards from the German assault in Europe and any hopes that we had for a quick end to the conflict were long forgotten. Like many men of my generation I had followed the progress of the war through the radio news broadcasts and the newspapers.

It seemed clear that the war effort was going to involve every able-bodied man. So, having registered as volunteer aircrew, I went home to wait for the call to arms and a couple of weeks later received instructions to make way to Uxbridge for a medical examination. I arrived on a Monday, two days after that unforgettable match at Selhurst Park that I told you about.

Assembling at Uxbridge with many other men from the south of England I soon found myself standing in line and waiting my turn to see the medical officer. To my amazement and disgust I failed the examination at almost the first hurdle. "Blood pressure too high Tarratt. Sorry, but we can't take a risk on you with flying duty. You'll have to have a job on the ground." was the gist of the message.

I was devastated. All my life I had been leading a healthy outdoor life and now my blood pressure was going to keep me from taking an active part in fighting the enemy. But leaving aside my anger and unhappiness I was now being pressed to make my mind up on the job I wanted, given that flying was no longer an option. I was presented with a long list of possible roles and scrolling down through the list I quickly decided to volunteer to train as a Physical Training Instructor.

I had always enjoyed PT, I was used to training routines and I knew I was fit and healthy – despite anything some "jumped-up" junior medic might decide to the contrary. Soon I was on my way to Bridgnorth in Shropshire for drill, basic weapons instruction, and drill, drill and more drill. After nearly two months of 'square-bashing' I was heartily sick of marching up and down so it was a blessed relief to get my travelling instructions and be on my way to Liverpool for what should have been seven weeks of PT instruction but turned out to be ten.

There were some fine chaps on the course, in particular I remember George Cox, who played for Arsenal and England. George and I became firm friends. It was a fully trained and fighting fit Ralph Tarratt who, having received my first posting, headed back south firstly to RAF Manston and then on to RAF Andover . I journeyed down by train and, having arrived in Kent, set off to the aerodrome.

Walking through the gates on a bright, clear afternoon I made way to the administration block and was puzzled at the remarkable absence of servicemen and officers. The place appeared to be deserted as I headed towards the canteen, thinking that if I could not find the duty officer and register my arrival at least I might find a cup of tea. Seconds later I heard the metallic scream of an aeroplane engine and looked up to see a dirty-grey fighter streaking toward me with all guns blazing. "Look out Ralph," I thought, "Jerry knows you're here even if nobody else does."

Dropping my cases I headed toward the nearest shelter. In a flying tangle of RAF greatcoat, boots and cap I clattered in through the big iron door. "Here, watch out," growled a grumpy mechanic, "You're more of a danger than those flippin' Huns". RAF Manston was under attack and would be again on the hour and every hour throughout daylight. As soon as the klaxon sounded every man and woman on the base would drop what they were doing and head at full speed for safety.

Losing the race for the shelters and ditches literally cost men their lives and this would not be the last time that I had cause to be grateful for being quick on my feet. But after a few weeks the air raids seemed to become more of an irritant than a threat and like some of the other lads I started to pay less attention to the sirens. One day I was having lunch and playing snooker in the NAAFI when the familiar whine of the klaxon started up. I was at the snooker table as the Germans flew in.

I had a good few points on the board and the colours were well set up for me to rack up a big break and win the game. So, as the sound of aeroplane engines mixed with the clatter and rattle of the anti-aircraft machine guns, I carried on potting. Just as I was lining up another red my mate and I heard the distinctive whistle made by a 500-pound bomb heading our way. Words were unnecessary as we slipped under the snooker table and held our hands over our ears.

There was a brilliant flash of light, the most enormous explosion, and then the table began to shake and shiver as first an iron girder and then hundreds of roof tiles came clattering down. "Jerry" has scored a direct hit on the NAAFI and the only thing that saved me from certain death was the slate bed that formed the base of the snooker table. As I crawled out from my temporary shelter I found the table makers nameplate lying amongst the rubble- "JELKES."

I think I might have said a little prayer for those craftsmen I had known who had built the table. Needless to say there was not much snooker played for a good while and whenever the air raid siren was heard in the months to come if Tarratt was not the first into the shelter he certainly wasn't far behind. I soon settled in at Manston and like everyone else longed for some leave and a chance to get home and see my family. But before I got to the top of the list I was posted on to RAF Andover.

It was another fighter aerodrome in continuous action. No sooner did I have my bearings and had become familiar with the routine of my job than the Sergeant in charge of transport, who knew I was a Horsham lad, offered me the chance of a ride on a lorry which was taking a captured Messerschmitt ME 109 single seat fighter up to the 49 M.U. at Faygate, not far from Horsham.

It seemed the aeroplane had run out of fuel and had crash-landed near Middle Wallop after a raid upon the aerodrome but all I really cared about was the possibility of it providing me with the transport needed for a quick trip home to the family. I got permission to take some leave, grabbed my kit bag and headed off to the waiting lorry. What I did not know was that I was not to be the only passenger on that journey and that the only seat remaining was the pilot's seat in the German fighter.

Nothing daunted, I clambered aboard and settled down for the long drive ahead. From my lofty perch I had a wonderful view over the hedgerows as the countryside rolled gently by, though I had to sit up high in the seat to peer over the steep sides of the cockpit. At about lunchtime the lorry stopped outside 'The Cricketers' pub on Wisborough Green. "Just going in for a quick bit of lunch," shouted up the driver as he and his mates headed into the pub, "You coming?"

"No thanks," I called back, "I'm fine here," knowing a full home-cooked meal was waiting for me as I was so near my home town and family. The pub was owned at that time by a Mr Saunders who used to play for Portsmouth Football Club but even the chance of catching up on a bit football gossip wasn't going to get me out of my seat. I was so looking forward to that wonderful home cooking.

So I settled back to wait and soon I could hear the chattering of small children, who I suppose had gathered around the lorry to gaze at the German aeroplane sitting upon its flat bed transporter. I knew the high cockpit surround concealed me from them and perhaps I dozed off for a little while. Then I heard the driver shouting to me from the pub "'Ere mate, you alright? Anything you want?" "No thanks," I replied, "I don't want to spoil my appetite."

Startled by this exchange between the airman and an apparently empty cockpit one of the children turned to his mate, gripped him excitedly by the elbow and shouted "There's a Jerry still in the 'plane and he doesn't half speak good English"!

Some weeks later I received the orders I had long been waiting for. I had applied for a posting to the Middle East, a place I had always wanted to visit, but instead I now learned I was going to Kenya. It could not be better as far as I was concerned, though. My journey began at the dead of night when I left Andover for Canterbury. When I arrived I found the station knee deep in servicemen.

We were all ordered onto another train, which, we soon learned, was to take us to Bristol. I joined in the scramble to find a seat and I was soon glad that I had. The train stopped time and time again with more soldiers and airmen boarding at each halt. Then two more engines were added to our train so we knew ours was going to be a long journey. On we went until one of the boys noticed that we were heading north, and nowhere near Bristol. "Where to now?" we wondered aloud.

The word came down the train to say we were on our way to Liverpool. But no. On and on we travelled through Preston and still heading north. Finally, after three days and nights, we stopped. The doors were thrown open and we were ordered out. Glasgow was before us. We soon got formed up and marched out of the railway station and straight into the docks, where we soon boarded a large ship that had a distinctly powerful smell about it. After a long day I was dog-tired.

I joined the scrum to grab enough space to fall down and sleep. Next morning was grey and dismal. Excited though I was at the thought of taking my first sea cruise I had no idea where we were heading or what was waiting for me at the other end. I joined in the speculation with all the lads who, like me, were wondering what lay in store. Our ship, the Highland Monarch, turned out to be a converted refrigeration ship, used until then to bring meat into Britain from overseas, which explained why we were all reminded of a butcher's shop.

Our ship slipped away from the dockside and took its position near the head of the convoy of some 40 ships, of all shapes and sizes. On board we learned there were some 900 men aboard, mostly RAF and from various trades. Despite the excitement of the moment most of the lads got their heads down on the open deck to sleep as best we could. We were "knackered" after four nights with hardly any sleep.

As the day wore on we were joined by other merchant ships and occasionally by a Royal Navy warship thrashing along in between the lumbering cargo vessels, reminding me of the collies we kept on the farm to help round up the cattle. The tranquility and beauty of Cox Farm where I had been brought up felt like a lifetime ago and a million miles away. As our convoy grew we could make out our escorts more clearly. We were in the company of three destroyers, a number of frigates, and the most enormous battleship.

The days rolled by. Eat, sleep, play games of cards, chat with new mates and gaze across the convoy towards the sun setting out to the left each night. That soon became the routine as we sailed to war. But this was to be no pleasure cruise and we were soon awoken by a loud "crunching" noise below deck. It became clear that we were losing ground quickly and soon we found ourselves near the rear of the convoy.

We had long lost sight of land and now the other ships in the convoy were mere dots on the horizon. Over the 'Tannoy' we were told that we were in the Bay of Biscay, that we had "lost" one of our engines and that our orders were to proceed to Freetown, where a replacement engine would be awaiting us. There was not any panic but none of us liked the idea of being left out alone in the middle of the ocean, with one of our engines useless.

It was a potentially dangerous situation and very worrying, but we grasped at the one small positive side to it all. On the one hand there was concern but on the other relief to know we were heading for shore and we could get off this stinking tub. However, Freetown was several days steaming away and we would be without any protection, apart from a small anti-aircraft gun situated on the after-deck of the "old crate." Our ship laboured on and twice we spotted "Jerry" planes overhead but fortunately they turned away, probably thinking we were already "goners".

Finally we reached our destination, but far from it being a pleasant place it was very humid. and a terrible smell hung over the harbour. It was a ghastly experience and we soon learned that it was noted as being one of the most likely places to catch malaria. But we deserved some good luck, we thought, and with a new engine fitted and after only six days in the stench and filth of Freetown, we were away again.

One remarkable memory of the trip was the sight of the flying fish – something I had never heard of and I still recall the amazing way they darted in and out of the sea, glistening in the sun. Whenever I saw them, it seemed to me to be a moment of great natural beauty in what was an ugly journey, and lifted my spirits a good deal. The rest of our voyage passed by without any problems and I have fond memories of the scramble to grab a place at the ship's rail to get a look at our final destination.

Table Mountain lay ahead of us, one of the landmarks of South Africa. The farmer's boy from Horsham had travelled across the Equator and landed at the very southern tip of another continent. I joined the rush to grab my kit and get ashore. "My first voyage," I remember thinking, "Not too bad." Of course, like people often do I was putting to the back of my mind what had gone before because I was so taken with the beauty of Cape Town.

The Cape Town people were warm hearted and friendly, taking us on trips and feeding us up with juicy steaks and gallons of beer. Ah, what a wonderful place it was. We were all ordered to assemble with our kit to march the two miles to the "tented" holding centre that covered a large area of ground. We had been worried the camp would be crammed full and we might have to sleep in the open. Nothing of the sort awaited us. At least three quarters of the camp was empty.

Any rate we were dead tired and settled down for the night. Probably every man slept well that night, the better for knowing that, owing to our late arrival, the morning parade and roll call would be at 9 o'clock. This was the life. The following morning, the parade over, we decided to explore the empty camp and to say the least we were somewhat perplexed. Here we were in a half empty camp in warm sunny weather and a long way from the war but the mood amongst the men already in camp was dark and sombre.

When the duty officer had addressed us on parade he seemed greatly disturbed and mentioned a recent tragedy, but we knew no more than that. We quickly discovered the NAAFI, which was sited in a large marquee, and sat down to enjoy a glass of the famous local lager. Already sitting alone at a table was a "squaddie" from the Tank Corps who proved to be very talkative and he explained the mystery.

It seemed he was on a ship that was part of a convoy that had left Avonmouth immediately before us and had suffered many losses. Although their convoy was a lot larger than the one we came on, they only had a battleship and two destroyers for protection. A few hundred miles down the African coast, they were attacked firstly by wave after wave of German bombers, and then strafed by many fighters who joined in the attack. The convoy was literally bombed out of the water with the battleship and a destroyer almost written off.

The remainder of the convoy struggled on, but after a few hundred miles of stuttering progress they fell right into the hands of a pack of U-boats. Those few ships that did survive the two attacks eventually got to Cape Town, and our new friend in the beer tent was clearly relieved and amazed to still be alive. The gloomy mood was all around us, and we decided the best thing was to get out of the camp and see the many sights awaiting us in the area.

Cape Town was a city catering for visitors, and with the favourable exchange rate between the pound and the rand and service personnel being charged only half price in the bars and cafes this was certainly a place to enjoy. Clearly the camp commander recognised this because they even permitted sleeping out passes. I was keen to visit the famous Garden Trail that runs between some of the most noted gardens in the world and it certainly lived up to its reputation.

Then we travelled by rail on long journeys up country, eating and sleeping on the train, and stopping off at gardens and places with wonderful views. Some of the gardens left us absolutely spellbound, with so many different species that were a total mystery to us then. Two friends joined me and it was a great start to our time abroad. We saw an excellent circus, visited Sea-world, a fine butterfly farm, a zoo, and had a day at the races.

This was truly a life of leisure while across the world war raged. A few of us went to the top of Table Mountain and the view was breathtaking. We borrowed two small tents so that we could stay overnight and enjoyed a night around the campfire exchanging stories about our lives at home in England. When we returned to camp in the late afternoon, however, there was a message awaiting me and I think I knew that the lazy days were over. I was to report to the RAF Office.

I learned I had orders to move off at five the following morning, take a Jeep and driver and make my way to my posting at Police Headquarters, three miles out of Nairobi.

Dawn the next day promised another sunny morning and a very long journey ahead. Two male nurses were travelling with me and it was quite a squash with our luggage on the roof. Away we went, driving through the spectacular African countryside, making several stops on the way.

Days later, we reached a very large and imposing hospital on the outskirts of Nairobi and no-one was more grateful than our driver who believed we had a slow puncture, and who was also unhappy with the engine, which was certainly firing badly. So I said goodbye to the two nurses and left the driver to find the hospital garage and get working on the Jeep. I managed to scrounge a cup of tea and some refreshments and took a walk around the grounds of the hospital that had been built within a large park.

I had already heard that it was regarded as the top hospital in Africa and was believed held to be second only to Aldershot, which was then rated the best military hospital in the world. All too soon a shout from the garage told me we were ready to go. I had much to think about as we headed into the city. During my short stroll in the hospital grounds I had stopped for a chat with a gardener who told me that the injured from the convoy, whose sad story I had heard of in the NAAFI canteen, had been flown to the hospital for surgery.

The survival rate was very small, and added to the known dead and the growing toll of bodies washed onto the shore, took the total number of dead troops to many hundreds. Now I knew that we had been lucky to make it in one piece to Cape Town and my thoughts were shared between sadness at the loss of so many fellow countrymen and nervousness as I contemplated the future.

We drove on through the city and it was almost midnight when we finally reported to the guardroom. I explained to the duty sergeant that the driver was tired out and needed a bed for the night so he phoned the duty officer who agreed that, rather than wake up the whole sleeping quarters, we could bed down in the guard room. And thoughtfully he warned the Adjutant that in view of my late arrival it would be quite late when I reported to him.

The pleasant stay in Cape Town seemed long ago and I was out on my feet, but could not sleep or get the thought of those terrible events out of my mind. Then, when I finally did drop off I had a vivid dream - something I seldom experienced and I could only think this one was heightened by the recent tragedy. My dream saw me in the Nairobi hospital I had visited that very day but now I was a casualty and not a visitor. Never having been one who believed in dreams coming true I put my fears behind me, or at least I tried to, but I confess there have been moments since then when the dream has come back to haunt me.

After this long and restless night, I got some breakfast, took a quick tour of the camp and headed off to see the station Adjutant. He was older than I had expected, probably a pilot from the last War as he wore the 'wings' and campaign ribbons. He said: "I hear you have quite a story to tell", rang a bell and his orderly brought in a pot of tea. He listened with keen interest as I told him of my trip from the south of England to Nairobi.

Reflecting upon the horrible loss of life I remember him sadly commenting that the result of Field Marshall Montgomery's many public appeals for more recruits may have been successful, but now most of them were at the bottom of the ocean. The truth was that out in Africa there was a desperate shortage of manpower, literally there was no one to man the equipment. The Adjutant was not a man to dwell on problems, I would find.

"I want you to join tonight's patrols, and tomorrow there's a job to do bringing in a prisoner from a local village." He went on: "I doubt if your next posting is many days away and my guess is it'll be in the desert where all hands will be required." I could see the plight they were in - it was all hands to the pump.

In fact it was three weeks to the day that my posting later came through and it was not the desert, but police headquarters in Cairo. We were to fly there by civil airline but in the last few days before I was scheduled to leave I managed to take in a few local attractions during the odd moments of time off. A bird park was fascinating but the crocodile farm was a frightening place. Understanding the threat and the power of the inmates did not need any imagination – the three keepers missing various arms or legs were evidence enough.

Nairobi was a fascinating city made up with its exotic mix of buildings, old and new. I was very taken with the city museum featuring breathtaking woodcarvings by elderly Africans. I marvelled at the skill and patience that must have been needed to create these masterpieces.

4 THE HOUSE OF ILL REPUTE

Finally, I was on my way to Cairo. My fellow passengers included a police corporal and several officers newly discharged from hospital. Our flight was unremarkable. We landed and I was directed to a Jeep and driven to RAF police headquarters in Cairo, where I was met by the duty sergeant, who showed me to my quarters. It was apparent that only about half the beds were occupied, probably by about 40 men. I unpacked my gear and found my way to the club bar where I met some of the lads and, after a few games of darts, turned in for the night.

After breakfast the following morning I decided to explore the station. It was a very imposing building, situated in its own grounds in the more salubrious part of the city. Before being commandeered for use by the RAF it had been a boys' boarding school. As I stood admiring the façade I suddenly felt a hand on my shoulder and, turning round, I jumped smartly to attention. It was the station Warrant Officer welcoming me to Cairo and apologising for being so long in seeing me.

He explained that he was snowed under with paper work but that if I would go to his office at 4pm the next day, we could have a long chat. I could not believe what was happening. Warrant Officers do not even talk to RAF aircraftsmen let alone apologise to them. It seemed there was something very strange going on. I asked some of the lads what they knew about him and they gave me some useful information. His name was Len Lowe, he was an ardent supporter of Cardiff City, dead keen on football and very young for his comparatively high rank.

That still did not explain his behaviour, however. So, promptly at 4 pm I presented myself at his office where he told me to sit down and tell him about myself. I explained that I had expected to be responsible for PT but I already realised that his staff were far too busy to be put under the extra pressure of having physical training added to their workload.

He confirmed that there was no chance of setting up a PT unit and, as the Adjutant was on leave until after the weekend, he was unable to tell me precisely what my duties would be. But, he went on, what he had in mind was for me to escort prisoners, a job which had fallen very much in arrears. He reiterated that he was heavily overloaded with paperwork and said that he had another job that needed doing.

He wanted me to take over his work at the local brothel. All British servicemen and officers stationed overseas were continually reminded to beware when "fraternising with the locals" and probably every one of us had heard stories of the horrible diseases that could be picked up from prostitutes. But, despite all the warnings, the daily sick parade would all too often see a queue of men who clearly had ignored the advice of the medics.

The military authorities, knowing that they could never prevent men chasing women, would instead unofficially "sanction" a brothel and to ensure nothing untoward would infect the visitors they would arrange for the girls who worked there to have regular health checks. In Cairo it seemed the Warrant Officer was required to look after the medical welfare and well-being of the girls working in the brothel, who were generally examined every seven days by Egyptian doctors.

Now it would be my responsibility to work with the "Madame", who had the same character as that of an English Matron and who ruled the place with a rod of iron. I soon learned that she would not put up with any drunkenness or rowdyism and any clients who did not toe the line were quickly shown the door. There were some 30 girls at the brothel, mostly Egyptians, who did shift work, 4 days a week for our troops, who were strictly forbidden to have anything to do with the street girls.

It was at breakfast the following day when there was an announcement over the Tannoy instructing me to report to the Adjutant's office immediately. A very blunt man, he came straight to the point, telling me that he was giving the Station Warrant Officer permission to do whatever was necessary to take over the medical work at the brothel. He had already collected that day's papers and would take me to meet Sally the next day at 10am and she would show me the ropes.

Right on time the next morning he was waiting in the brothel's courtyard where, after making the necessary introductions, he left me to the tender mercies of the portly "Madame" who proceeded to give me a guided tour of the brothel and show me the girls' rooms. These were quite different from anything I had imagined and were exotically furnished with Eastern drapes and curtains. There were three slightly larger rooms specially set aside for officers.

The girls seemed to be very ordinary young Egyptians and very easy to talk to. I thanked "Madame" for showing me around and promised to return the next morning. On arriving back at HQ I ran into Len and thanked him for the trouble he had taken. He had had my bed moved into a small room off the main dormitory and I was gratified to find that everything was in order and that I even had a telephone of my own.

That night I turned in early but found to my horror in the morning that I was covered in red spots. I had failed to check the legs of my bed, which should have stood in tins of paraffin that were the only means of preventing an invasion of biting bed bugs. In the two and a half months during which I was responsible for the medical records there was only one case of infection, which fortunately turned out to be a scare, although it caused a panic in the brothel at the time.

I was looking after the blooming medical side, not that I knew much about medicine, with the prostitutes. I had to make sure they were medically examined. Thank heavens, I did not check them. I just had to make sure the doctor came in and checked them. And some of them were nice girls, attractive-looking girls. But the authorities were so afraid of VD.

Soon it was back to football again, and the meeting of the Cairo FA committee, of which Len was vice-chairman. There were some 30 or so members present, comprising service personnel and some Egyptians, and Len chaired the meeting of representatives from the five zones, each sending two delegates. The League had been founded several years earlier and initially had very much resembled our own village set-up, but the arrival of the services had enlarged the Association tremendously.

It was then, in the searing heat thousands of miles from home, that I came across the names of teams like Chelsea and Arsenal again.

A strange rule passed at the formation of the local League and insisted on by the founder members was that clubs should be named after English clubs. For example, the marines club was called Chelsea and so on. The British forces had ploughed in a great deal of money, which had been used to improve the grounds and facilities and as a result the Association was fortunate enough to own two of the best grounds in the whole of Africa.

The Alamein and Gaza clubs both employed their own groundsmen who were responsible for watering the pitches every day and all inter-league fixtures were played at their two grounds. The subject of referees was brought up early in the meeting and I was formally elected as a member of the committee. It transpired that my job was to coach new referees.

There was a severe shortage of competent referees and a sergeant major offered to arrange for a number of FA rule books to be typed and printed in both English and Egyptian. A quick glance at the list of referees revealed that none had reached football league standard but that most of them had had experience with either the Southern Midland or the Football Combination. Quite a lot were over the age limit and some were inevitably only occasionally available for matches, being committed to the duties of their official posting.

We retired to the bar where the chat was about the forthcoming visit of the "Wanderers" which was a team of touring professional footballers, including some England internationals sent all over the place to be a tonic for the troops. I was surrounded by quite a few of the referees who asked various questions and I soon found I had to be very careful about what I said. They wanted their own way and made it clear which match they would prefer to be in charge of, and other things, so I had to be firm.

We said our "Cheerios", and Len was so pleased at how the meeting had gone and dropped me off saying: " I see your measles have almost gone - never forget the paraffin" Of course by 'measles' he meant my insect bites and no, I never forgot to check the levels in the paraffin tins again. Things were getting back to normal and I had made a hole in the number of prisoners to be brought in.

One very interesting prisoner I had to escort was making headlines in both the English and local papers. He was a Brigadier who had been arrested by Military Police and charged with shooting a Wren officer of high parentage in a hotel bedroom. I had to travel to pick him up and I could not have wished to meet a nicer man. I did not escort him at the court marshal, and unfortunately having left Cairo a few days after the case was heard I never got to hear the outcome.

On the football front things were moving along fine. My first training session had 17 candidates, all very keen and quite young. A male nurse from the hospital and an Egyptian pal assisted in the training. I was unable to attend the next committee meeting as it clashed with an escort job, but I gathered that Len, who chaired the meeting, told them in no uncertain terms that I was by far the most senior referee to join their Association. It was a blessing I was absent or I would have been embarrassed. But he never mentioned to me putting in that good word, because he was that sort of man.

I was getting ready for supper when my telephone rang - it was Len. He said:

"I have to go out this evening - will you stand in for me? Our Commanding Officer wants to have a chat with our officer prisoner." They had been buddies together since college and the policy was that someone had to be present in the prison cell. He said: "Put cotton wool in your ears. I will advise the C.O. and he will ring you when ready."

The call came, I had already collected the key to the cell, and we met in the cell doorway where he greeted his chum. After a long chat, they shook hands and we left. This was the first time I had met the C.O. He thanked me for being discreet. He had only taken a few steps when he called me back and said: "I expect you have heard the rumours about the leakage of petrol down south - well, you have been selected to lead a party of eight to look into the problem."

Losing nine of our staff certainly created great difficulty. "Owing to the urgency, you will be leaving in a matter of a few hours. Tomorrow the Warrant Officer will fill you in with more details. Good luck". Very early next morning the call came from Len and he said: "Now you know you are leaving us we will discuss the details. I have already selected the eight" and he told me their names. I asked if it was possible to make one change in the list of names.

There was one man on our staff who I very much wished to accompany me - Corporal Frost, who had had two years in the S.I.B. Midlands Police. Without further ado he said: "Your instructions are that you will be taken by road to Port Said and from there you will be given orders on how you will proceed to Mombassa." Arriving at the docks at Port Said, we checked in and the naval officer in charge said that our ship was due to sail at noon. We scoured the dockland area but could see no sign of a British naval vessel.

Finally we were directed to the other side of the docks where our ship was berthed. It was a real rust bucket - even the name was indistinguishable. Still, orders were orders. We made our way in the direction indicated and as there was no one around we climbed on board and eventually a tall Indian man who spoke good English announced that he was the Captain. He also appeared to be the worse for drink, close to mid-day.

He took us to our sleeping quarters and asked whether we preferred hammocks or bunks. With one voice we declared "hammocks" because in the few minutes we had been on board we realised the ship had rats scurrying all over the place. Slipping away from the quayside we were soon at sea, our first call being at Eritrea to pick up a load of rope. We went ashore and our feet had hardly left the gangplank when we were surrounded by children rattling tin cans, who appeared to be starving.

We made a brief tour of the area, consisting mostly of shantytowns, and hurried back on board thoroughly depressed with the sights we had seen. Soon we were away down the Suez Canal heading for the open Ocean. Every night the crew held a singsong of Indian Shanties, drinking pints of their special brew. What concerned me was, despite travelling in a fast and busy shipping lane, none of the crew seemed in a fit state to take watch on the bridge, leaving us wide open to a disastrous collision.

But luck was on our side and we continued slowly to make our way down the coast, stopping to pick up and drop our cargo. In all we made seventeen stops. One night, when we had all fallen asleep, there was a terrible screech. It was the chilling sound of one of the crew falling down the hatch, instantly breaking his neck, and sadly, he died. There was nobody capable of giving medical help - there wasn't even a first aid box on board.

Coming to our last call before disembarking, I thanked the skipper for his assistance and said that we had enjoyed the food and got used to the Indian cuisine, but he said that this wasn't their last call as they had to go on to Madagascar to pick up a consignment of tea. I said to him: "Can I give you an order?" to which he replied: "Yes, but I don't have to obey it." I then explained that we were days behind with our operation and so it would be very helpful if he could drop us off first.

He thought for a minute, and with the usual Indian grin gave the OK but said that he would expect a few hundred 'Camels', the popular cigarettes. Luckily only two of our lads smoked, so we were able to oblige him with a few cartons. Mombassa was a wonderful place and I was further delighted to find that we had been billeted in a rather handsome hotel, so I slept well that night. Waking up after a deep sleep in the rather strange dormer-like room was quite a shock; it reminded me of school days.

I had overslept and it was quite late. In walked a tall well-dressed African. He said: "Welcome. I'm the proprietor.   I run the hotel with my brother. You are the first occupants of this room. When the RAF first booked you in we cleared what was a food warehouse and turned it into this. As you have had no time to get organised I am laying on breakfast, which is on the house. Porridge, eggs bacon, and the rest. Round up your chaps and be in the dining room at 11.30 a.m."

When we entered, to my surprise I found that the three from the station were already there. "Smithy" said that it had been quiet night and that everything had been "sorted". All the vehicles were in the car park. This was great news and I thanked them for exceeding my expectations. The server asked how many wanted "seconds" and quite a few found room somehow. Then the girls arrived with dishes of various fruits, a cheese board followed, some of which I had never seen before. If that was a second-class commercial hotel, I wondered what the Grand at Brighton would dish up.

I told the lads to have a walk to shake down their breakfasts and warned them to be back in the room set aside for the meeting within an hour, for a council of war. They should put on their thinking caps and come up with ideas. I opened the proceedings by saying that we were weeks behind our unknown enemy. On the next day, Monday, we would take a day off to explore the area and I said that it was essential that I had a second in command.

With his police experience Corporal Frost was the obvious choice and this was agreed. On Tuesday we would show our strength by parading our vehicles around the main streets, and we would do this mid-morning every day to show that we meant business. Some of the others came up with different suggestions, which would be used as we progressed. I suggested to Frosty that we should go and see what transport had been allotted to us.

My eyes rested on a small jeep, which was almost brand new - right up my street. It would be great to get behind the wheel again. There was also a long wheel base jeep and two motor cycles, a powerful "Zenith" and a light weight Douglas plus two push bikes. The large lorry containing our 10-man tent, two smaller tents, cooking gear and everything else that was required was safely parked in the hotel grounds.

The two African lads had been allocated a small house at the rear of the hotel. I was itching to try out the jeep and he suggested that we should take a trip around the town. We spent the next couple of hours getting acquainted with the area and visiting a few of the mud-hut villages in the north of the town. Whilst having a drink at the bar before turning in, I mentioned to Frosty that, although I had said that the next day should be a day off, I wanted to call at the office of the local newspaper to see the manager and asked him if he was game to come along.

Although the manager was likely to be busy on a Monday, we agreed to call on him at about 10 a.m. The next morning we arrived at the newspaper office and asked the girl at the desk if we could make an appointment to see the editor. She telephoned him and was told that he had a client with him but if we were willing to wait, he would see us afterwards. In due course we were shown in and introduced to Bill Fletcher, the editor and joint proprietor.

He asked why it had taken us so long to contact him when the crime had taken place at least two months earlier. He said that the town was proud of being a crime-free environment and resented any slur on its good name. I explained the difficulties we had had in travelling from Cairo. He said that the whole area was behind us and that we would have their full support. I had already apologised for bursting in on him on a very busy day but, to my surprise, he said that we could not have timed things better.

He said: "I'm a Londoner and, not to beat about the bush, it is vital that our readers get the news without delay." The English edition was due on the streets on the following Monday. On Wednesday we would have the entire front page for our cause, and this would be in colour. The African version would come out at the weekend. It took my breath away. He said that he would want a brief pen picture of each one of my lads, including the two Africans.

He would arrange for a photographer to be at the hotel at 8 am on Monday - they had a very colourful front garden. I mentioned that our first show of strength around the town would be on Monday at about mid-day, but he suggested we made it earlier, so that photographs of vehicles and personnel could be included. He added that market day was a good day for a parade because all the surrounding villages piled in for the occasion.

I said that I could not thank him enough for all his help and that I looked forward to working together with him on the project. As we shook hands I suddenly remembered that I had not mentioned posters - did he know of a printer? He said that I was looking at one. I said that a substantial reward would be paid for information leading to an arrest. He said that I should leave that to him - he was used to writing and editing and that my posters would be ready for Monday's parade.

This episode had a curious ending. An informant told us how to catch the people we were after, but the military police arrested him instead. There now followed ten very happy months during which Cairo HQ presumably assumed we were still on the trail of the thieves and I didn't feel too inclined to inform them otherwise.

I set up some goalposts and ran training sessions and we even got some teams together and formed a league structure. For the winners of the cup competition we staged I was given a beautiful carved wooden trophy, immediately christened 'The Tarratt Trophy'. Many years afterwards I heard that the trophy was still in existence. Mrs Topham, the oncologist at the Crawley hospital who treated Joy, my third wife, with chemotherapy for her ovarian cancer told me that a nurse in the hospital, who came from Mombassa, had a football-crazy father who said it was displayed at Mombassa's Harbour Club.

Those were wonderful times but I knew that the authorities would catch up with news that the petrol thieving had stopped and so I was ordered back to Cairo. The return journey was truly memorable. I flew directly from Mombassa in a Shorts Sunderland flying boat. Right along the course of the Nile we flew, often at tree top level. It was a wonderful experience and the memory of watching elephants bathing as we hurtled overhead is one I have always cherished.

5   LOCUSTS AND HEARTBREAK

The wartime Wanderers football team was touring the area where I was serving, if you can call it serving because I was hardly seeing front line action and considered I was extremely lucky. Two thirds of the players on the Wanderers tour came from the UK. The 'stars' included Rayner, the Aldershot goalkeeper; Joe Mercer, who was to become Footballer of the Year in 1950, and Tom Finney, the celebrated winger from Preston North End who was one of Britain's finest players ever, and who, like Mercer, won England international caps.

Of course, all the lads knew the team was coming to North Africa because it was the talk of the mess, but I did not expect to be any more involved than as a spectator. So it came as a surprise when I was contacted directly by Joe Mercer who asked me if I would be willing to join the party and referee all their tour matches – assuming he could swing it with HQ of course. It seemed that one of the local referees had taken charge of the first match that the Wanderers had played on Egyptian soil, when they had taken on the Cairo Police.

The British boys were not too certain that he understood the rules of the game. Some of the tackling that he had turned a blind eye to had left them fearing permanent injury and they were anxious to ensure that future matches would be under the control of someone with greater experience. Their idea was to take a referee along with them on the tour and they wanted my O.K before they approached the authorities.

Who was I to say no, I thought, and when got it round that I was being posted to join the Wanderers tour party the lads in the mess were positively green with jealousy. As it was to turn out the tour was a bit of a "skive" for all concerned. The players, some sixteen or seventeen of them I think there were, all came from regiments of the British Army and most were officially posted as PT Instructors.

Some had been professional players before the War, but the majority of them were amateurs and a few were lacking in even basic fitness.

Clearly the War Office viewed the team as ambassadors sent to 'wave the flag' as they toured from country to country. The lads in the tour party didn't much care what they were classified as. Just as long as their billets were comfortable, there was plenty of good "grub" on offer with an occasional beer or three thrown in, and the opposition didn't get excited and take any of the matches too seriously. The 'Wanderers' were out to have a nice peaceful tour and I could see from the very first match that life as the team's official referee wasn't likely to offer too many challenges.

We had one remarkable game in Mombassa, having travelled there by aeroplane from Durban. It was a trip I had been looking forward to, having been stationed there for the "Great Petrol Robbery" when I had made a good pal. I cannot recall his name after so long now, but I remember that he was a tea planter, a Geordie lad by birth, who, having settled in Africa, had married a local girl and now they had two lovely daughters.

They employed some 400 workers and had built up a successful plantation, but he had always missed his football, so had decided to start his own league. He had levelled the ground, grown and trimmed a good grass pitch and constructed a pavilion alongside the touchline. If it was not quite St. James' Park at Newcastle it was certainly a fine little ground that he was rightly proud to have built. Having the 'Wanderers' play there was quite an occasion and the ground was packed with spectators.

Not many referees are forced to stop matches by locusts in their career, but I was about to get my chance. Well into the game, mid-way through the second half I think it was, what looked like a huge black cloud headed for the ground. Only this cloud was alive and of biblical proportions. Locusts, although relatively small, can be one of the most devastating forces of nature. This lot seemed to be like a flying carpet.

It was a bizarre spectacle to me as I tried to concentrate on the game in the baking heat and dazzling sunshine. Hundreds of thousands of the flying creatures came in at about roof height like a looming swarm of fighters attacking out of the sun. It had about the same effect as an eclipse of the sun as far as continuing the match was concerned. These things, I was told, could fly at a height of up to 600 ft and make 30 miles a day. I wished they would, because they were just above the pitch and it appeared they wanted to hang around.

Caught in the middle of this massive swarm of ugly flying bugs, things felt extremely unpleasant. I wondered what the hell was happening. It was absolutely as black as night out there for a while.

I reached for the old Thunderer whistle amid the chaos, halted the game, and told the players to shelter in the dressing room. I need hardly have bothered because faced with this seething wall of deeply unsettling creatures players were already preparing to get off the pitch.

We stayed off the pitch for ten minutes and the living cloud moved on. Or at least some of it did.

We came back on to the pitch with the boots of players sounding as if they were treading on Rice Krispies. A carpet of dead or dying locusts littered the pitch. I suppose they had collided with each other, I am not sure. Anyway we played on, but it was a mind-boggling thing for the foreigners over there who had never seen such a thing to experience it on such a scale.

I don't recall much else about that game, I think the football was pretty unremarkable, but to this day I have never forgotten the sight of those menacing locusts. I did about ten matches with the Wanderers. I was promoted to flight sergeant for the duration so that I could eat and drink in their mess with them, but I got no extra pay. It was a sort of honorary thing for me as referee. The Wanderers had a few good players, but to be honest they weren't very fit.

They were well looked after and sometimes they ate like pigs. One of two of them were resting on their reputations before the war. I was a lot fitter than they were, but I enjoyed refereeing their matches and the crowds liked to see them. Sadly for me my time with the team was cut short by an accident that left its legacy later in my life, triggering, I believe, the severe arthritis that I have to live with today.

Rayner, the Aldershot goalkeeper I mentioned earlier, had persuaded me, against my better judgement, that I should accompany him on a climbing trip in the foothills outside Nairobi. His cousin had opened a climbing centre and made such a fuss about it in the local rag and some of us went out.

Being a Sussex lad and used to gentle rolling hills, the mountains were pretty foreign country to me but rather than stick to my gut feeling to avoid the trip, off we went. I had never climbed in my life. We had not been climbing for more than an hour when I slipped. The rope had snapped. It cut itself on the ledge. His equipment was bloody awful. I grabbed the first thing that came to hand and felt a searing pain in my shoulder.

I was in agony and the support party had to help me back down and to the transport we were using. There was blood pouring from deep cuts on my right hand where I had been scrabbling to get a grip but I knew instinctively that it was my shoulder where the real damage had been done. The party set off back to Nairobi and dropped me at the hospital. The casualty department had me stuffed full of painkillers in a moment and I was instructed that I would be confined to bed for two days to prevent any danger of aggravating the damage.

By the following morning I was sitting up and watching life in the hospital ward. We went to number five hospital in Kenya and the amazing part was a little nurse who worked on my elbow said: " Ralph you come from Horsham don't you, do you know Dr Sparrow?" I said: "God yes." because when I worked for a dentist I was right next door to where he kept his horses in North Street. The nurse said: "Well, he's coming down to see you. "

He kept me there for five weeks. I remember he was a brilliant artist. I used to go out with him for the day and he would draw anything. It seemed that nurse had seen my papers when I had been registered as a patient and spotted the possible Sussex connection between me and the now Colonel Sparrow who was resident in the hospital.

The Colonel later arranged for me set up some gym classes for the hospital staff. It was nothing too strenuous but he agreed it was a good idea to make use of the fact that he had a trained a PT instructor sitting around with nothing to do. That was fine by me. Since the 'Wanderers' had left me behind to carry on their tour I was without orders, and until HQ caught up with me I could do nothing but sit out my time in the hospital and wait for further instructions.

That is the only time I was able to teach PT. The nurses, well most of them, were English girls, and we lived on the fat of the land. We ate beautiful food. They put on so much weight that one day I had said to Dr Sparrow: "Why don't you have a gym? He agreed, and they used to come down there, I could not do much because of my elbow, and they absolutely used to love it. I had a lovely job for a while. They were very pretty ladies.

It was later that I learned that Colonel Sparrow had a practice in North Street. In fact, I worked out we must been near neighbours during my time terrifying dental patients at Ellis Kent. All this came out when the opportunity came one morning for us to chat about our shared experiences of life back home. He was a keen amateur artist and one morning I got a call asking if I would care to join him on a walk into the bush where he planned to spend the day painting. There was a price to pay of course – he needed a hand carrying his easel.

We had a pleasant day together and over the weeks we often travelled together on day trips. He knew both my mum and dad and after the War he and I met up several times in Horsham. I am no artist but I like his paintings. Only a couple of years ago I went for lunch in the St. Peter's Restaurant, next to the church in Cowfold, and hung on the walls were several of the Colonel's paintings. Happy days. But life wasn't always a bed of roses, far from it and out there in the heat tragedy was never far away.

Many of the patients used to bathe in the stream that ran alongside the hospital on its way to the sea. On a sunny day it was often crowded with servicemen, sunning themselves or taking a swim. One afternoon, as I sat at the beach reading, I heard the most terrible scream.

Like everyone else I looked up to see someone thrashing the water like a man possessed. There was a horrible pink tinge to the usual muddy brown colour and suddenly I saw the tail of a crocodile emerge and break the surface of the water.

Several men nearest the water's edge rushed forward and grabbed the poor victim of the crocodile's attack. The creature made off and the lads brought the body ashore. He had a horrible stump where his left leg should have been and was bleeding profusely. Sadly, he died a few days later after gangrene poisoned his body. He was in the next bed to mine and when his end came I was cradling him in my arms as we waited for a nurse to get to us. But it would not have mattered because nobody could have saved him. He was a merchant seaman, a nice bloke by all accounts, and I wish now that I had known his name.

When the war ended I was one of the thousands of British and Commonwealth lads who celebrated the end of hostilities on distant shores, a long way from home. We had lived on rumours, official news and informed gossip for many a month so we knew that the Allies were making inroads into France, the Low Countries, Italy and Germany. 'Jerry' had long since been thrown back from his

North African adventure but it was hard to fathom out how well the war was going and pointless to speculate on when we might expect to go home.

There was also the war in the East to worry about. Singapore and Burma, these were just place names to us then, we had no idea of the horrors that our lads were experiencing in those far-flung lands. Our only fear was that some bright-eyed 'Herbert' in some anonymous department of the War Office might dream up a posting for us somewhere other than dear old Blighty, a prospect too awful to joke about.

But when it came to my turn to get the call to head home it was in strange and ultimately heartbreaking circumstances that made it very hard to bear, and the episode all began on the football pitch. After I came out of hospital someone else looked after the brothel. I carried on with the police, helping them and doing odd jobs. One of the many games I had to referee was the officers playing the office staff for the division cup.

The Commanding Officer, who was playing at right-back, had been in the very thick of it. When he kicked seven bells out of some poor opponent for the second time I realised things could only get worse. My whistle never seemed to leave my mouth as I blew up for foul after foul. What had made me more nervous as I waited to see him was that the officers had wanted the carnage to continue.

When I had decided to call a halt before someone lost a limb it had been to the relief of the team of clerical staff but not to the officers, who seemed to think the whole thing was just one great giggle. What I didn't know at that time was that the officers had spent the half hour before the match downing what we called "pinkers" better known as 'Pink Gins', which were made of extremely large measures of gin and a couple of drops of Angostura Bitters.

Led by their gallant C.O. the whole team was totally "plastered." Little wonder then that they were hurling themselves around like whirling dervishes. They were quite oblivious to pain, having pickled their tiny minds with a case of Gordon's finest export strength gin. The C.O. was also a good rugby player and being tough, he was tackling blokes right, left, and centre. I had only one linesman anyway, and he was not really a proper linesman, he was only an office chap.

The cause of the stupidity on the pitch was not my concern however but what I had to ensure was that matters did not get any further out of hand. So far the clerks had kept themselves in check, but it was pretty clear that if the officers continued to kick lumps out of them there would be a limit to their patience and I would be refereeing a bloodbath. I had to do something, and I blew for half-time about ten minutes before I should have done and I thought to myself: "I don't think this game can be finished."

With my heart in my mouth I knocked on the dressing room door of the officer's team and asked for a word with the Adjutant. He said: "I think I know why," guessing the reason for my call, which couldn't have been too hard for him. I knew him to be a sensible sort of a bloke so I explained that his team had to calm down but that in my view the C.O. was completely out of order and they should leave him in the dressing room when play resumed and finish the match with ten men. He took a moment to think it through but I could see he knew that I was right.

Anyway the C.O. came over to me and I said: "Look sir, do you mind not taking the field in the second half? He said something to the effect: "Who the hell are you to tell me that?" although I must say he was a very nice man when he was sober. Anyway I steeled myself a bit and I said to him: "Will you please NOT take the field, otherwise I am going to call the game off."

And so, when the teams appeared for the second half the C.O. was not to be seen and the officers fielded one player short. I put the incident to one side but a few weeks later it returned to haunt me in heartbreaking fashion. I was very much of a pal with my warrant officer who was football mad. He brought the mail round, which we used to get every week. I had not heard from Billie for two or three months and we used to write quite a lot. I smelt a rat.

But that fateful letter from my wife seemed at first glance to be no different from any of the many others that Billie had written since I had been overseas. She wrote of everyday life in the town, of day-to-day events, of friends and family. But then it took a sad twist. Billie had met a sailor. She said she was ecstatic; they were in love and had set up home in Horsham, so why didn't I forget about coming back and instead make a new life for myself in Egypt? I could not believe my eyes.

All thoughts of resuming our life together summarily dismissed. No words of comfort; no regrets; no 'ifs' or 'maybes' just a cold, hard and almost formal proposal that I remove myself from our world together and leave her free to bring this new man into her life. I took the news very badly but fortunately the first person to come across me as I sat trying to cope with this awful mess was Len, who had become more of a mate than a Warrant Officer whose word was law.

We talked things through and it became clear to me that I needed to get home just as quickly as possible and see what I could do to retrieve the situation. Rightly or not I could not conceive our marriage ending on the strength of Billie's letter and I knew I needed to look her straight in the eyes if I was ever to know if she had any feelings left for me. Len, bless him, agreed and took the letter, offering to show it to the Squadron C.O. who was the only officer able to get me home.

Who said what to whom behind the dressing room door three weeks before I did not care to know, but I had not seen the C.O. since that infamous day of the football match and I was not much looking forward to the next time we met. Now, as well as having to face the possible wrath of the most powerful officer in the camp, I needed him to do me a huge and very personal favour. My future was looking far from rosy.

The following day at 3pm. I was up before the C.O. I was more uncertain than ever about what fate might have in store for me and all the recent events were tumbling through my mind as I stood rigidly to attention in front of his office desk. But his uncertain manner was far from what I had expected. He mumbled a few words then said: "Look Tarratt, sit down." It was unheard of. Me, a sergeant seated in the presence of my C.O.

I saw on his desk the letter the warrant officer had passed to him, which said in effect: "Don't ever come home again. I have found a lovely man." In a measured tone that put me a little more at ease he said he had reflected carefully on the infamous football match. He said he thought I was right to act as I did, and he recognised he had been at fault. He went on to explain that he and the other officers were all very aware of the many problems faced by officers and men who were all too often receiving difficult news from home.

He said he respected that problems with wives and sweethearts were private problems but the warrant officer had spoken with him about me and he wanted to help. He was making arrangements for me to be posted home on compassionate leave but it would take a couple of days to pull all the necessary strings. So, in the meanwhile, I was to take a car and a driver from the transport pool and make my way, over the next three days, to Alexandria where I should expect to receive my orders to take a ship directly to Liverpool.

I was overwhelmed but I think he was just relieved. He was probably a kindly man who certainly didn't have to put himself out to help me, anymore than he had to confess to being out of order on a football pitch. But, that said, I don't think he relished the prospect of me amusing all my mates with the story of the C.O.'s confession of bad behaviour, so getting me away from the camp as quickly as possible gave him the comfort of knowing that his dignity would be retained, in the sergeants mess at least.

He said to me: "They will all think you have gone up the desert." He was as sober as a judge then, behaving like a lovely bloke and being entirely reasonable about a delicate situation. I jumped to my feet, thanked him for his kindness, gave him my smartest salute, made a perfect parade-ground right turn, and marched out of his office. An hour later, I had my kit bag packed, had said: "Good-bye and good luck" to my mates and was in a car and away.

Unlike the outward journey, my return sea voyage was almost a pleasure cruise. The ship was packed with servicemen all anxious to be home with many a tale of derring-do ready to tell their wives and children and, indeed, anyone who would listen. I do not suppose we really thought much about what life might have been like for those we had left at home but I certainly looked forward to getting home with very mixed feelings.

It would be wonderful to see my parents, our relations, and all my old mates, but over-riding these happy thoughts were my concerns about Billie and the fate of our marriage. We docked at Liverpool one morning and I joined the throng crowding to leave the ship. We made our way along the quayside to where we were to pick up our orders. When I reached the head of the queue imagine my amazement to find an arm slipped around my shoulders as I leafed through the sheaf of orders I had received.

It was my greatest pal, George Cox, who had been put in charge of billeting. What a wonderful surprise it was to see him. We greeted one another like long-lost brothers as he told me how he had learned that I was en-route for "Blighty" and had managed to get some leave to come up to Liverpool to find me. What a pal. He was a Horsham lad too, but whereas I had donned the black shirt of the referee, he had been wearing the red shirt of the 'Gunners' his footballing career having taken him to dizzy heights at the Arsenal.

Not only that, he'd also won his full County cap as a regular first team player for Sussex County Cricket Club. Thankfully he'd come back from the War in one piece, ready to take up his place in the team and lead them to new triumphs. He had spent a lot of his time as bomber crew flying Lancasters. So many lads never returned but, thankfully, George was spared and he would go on to take his place playing football for England, where his performances on the pitch were a delight to thousands of supporters.

One of my proudest moments would come years later when I had the privilege of refereeing George's testimonial match at Horsham. Star players of their day were happy to turn out to benefit one post war England's finest players and I confess I had a tear in my eye when I blew the whistle for the close of play. But for now he was just the best of mates who had arranged for the two of us to spend a couple of nights in Blackpool, where we could catch up on each other's news.

We arrived at our boarding house late that night and when I found my way to the dining room for breakfast the next day there was my brother, Harry. George had arranged that too, without telling me a thing. We three had a high old time. Harry was in the RAF too, at that time serving as a mechanic at Middle Wallop. He knew from mum and dad that things between Billie and me were not as they should be, but it was all news to George and I think he was very saddened when he learned what had happened.

All to soon the party was over and we went our separate ways. Because I had been returned home on compassionate leave, I had been given a posting to RAF Tangmere, in order to be close to home. My reunion with my parents was wonderful but not so with Billie. From the first moment it was obvious that she was fully committed to her new life and that she and I had no future together. Sad, but I think I knew I was probably wasting my time trying to patch things up between us.

When I got back to Horsham, at Denne Park the big house there was full of Canadian officers. There must have been about 40 of them. I heard Billie used to go out with another girl or two girlfriends. Then she met a local man who had been discharged from the Navy. To take the story forward a little we were eventually divorced at Lewes in 1947. The grocery shop we ran in Park Street Horsham was soon closed and became a jewellers.

I heard as this book was being prepared that Billie had died. In fact, she outlived my second and third wives, who both fell victim to cancer. I had been drawn to Billie because we shared an interest in tennis and she was a pretty little thing. But the "Dear John" letter she sent me and the heartbreaking words it contained will always be one of the lowest points of my life.

When we divorced, as with any married couple that decide to part, there were practical issues to address, not least the future of the bar billiards business we had worked on together before I had left for the RAF. Now I found I was in for another surprise. It seemed that the wartime government, anticipating the problem that thousands of discharged service personnel would cause to the labour market, had guaranteed to the civilians then in work that none of them would lose their jobs to those now returning to 'Civvy Street'.

So, like it or not, Billie was quite within her rights to insist that she could keep sole control of the bar billiards business for the next two years. Like it or lump it, I was out of work as well as out on my ear.

6   A NEW START

After the war I did various jobs at times to make a living, before I was able to later concentrate fully on the bar billiards business on my own account. For a couple of years after I got back and Billie temporarily continued her bar billiards "round " I worked for the table maker Jelkes, selling tables into premises.

In the middle of all this I organised a bar billiards competition when local butcher and Sussex cricketer George Pearce and chairman of the local council Stan Parsons challenged the well-known bar billiards players the Davis brothers. It packed the Drill Hall in Horsham, and made a lot of money for Horsham Hospital.

The grocery store was eventually closed after my split with Billie and to help make a living I also sold all kinds of ladies clothes as an agent for a Liverpool firm, Greydear I believe they were called, also undertaking a similar line of clothing work for Ashpool and Twiddey of Leicester.

Later, on my rounds, by an astonishing coincidence that perhaps neither of us would have looked for, I went into a shop in New Milton and who should be running it but Billie. We were polite, but there was not nearly enough warmth between us by then for there to be any possibility of us getting together again.

When I handled an Everton-Liverpool match two of the clothing firm's directors were on the board and watched the game. Afterwards they made me southern "rep". But what really got me on my feet was having the agency for "pacamacs" the rainwear clothing. When I left to concentrate on the bar billiards business I was still getting commission on that for about four years, which really helped the bank balance.

I knew one of the directors of Southampton Football Club and he asked me what I was doing for a living. When I told him I was a rep he said: "I think I can help you." He got me permission to go on the steamers and boats. There was a marvellous market on the boats, and that's where the repeat orders for the "pacamacs" came from. That agency brought me in a hell of a lot of money." Selling skirts, blouses, underwear and the like as a "traveller," as they used to call them in those days, kept the money coming in, too.

As business picked up towards the turn of the decade after the war ended, the way to Sussex Bar Billiards being set up in 1954 was paved initially by me asking my "boss" Mr Sherlock for a rise, for my considerable efforts in getting more tables placed and of course collecting. Mick, one of the sons of my second wife Edith, was repairing the table clocks for Sherlock, and remembers he reacted by offering to sell me the business, although it did not immediately become Sussex Bar Billiards under my control.

I have already mentioned in an earlier context some of the post-war football matches but there are several others that stick in my mind to this day. The years 1946 to 1950 were described as the boom years for professional football, with huge crowds paying their equivalent of 6p in modern money (one shilling and three pence) to watch from the packed open terraces. The game was so popular that many people "skived" off work to watch to avoid the drudgery of their existence as society endured rationing long after the war finished and people worked long hours with fewer holidays.

Saturday afternoon except for the summer was for watching football, even if not all of it that was played immediately post-war was enthralling. This was half a century or so before television executives started dictating to clubs about when clubs played matches. In those days football fans knew their team would be kicking off at 3pm on Saturday and all they had to do was click their way through the turnstiles to see their heroes.

It was a long way from today's 5pm kick-offs, Sunday matches, pre-booked tickets and club memberships, although I remember facilities at a lot of grounds were pretty spartan, even if the fans didn't seem to mind that much. Enthusiasm for football was sometimes astonishing. Remember there was no such thing as an all seater covered club stadium and thousands simply stood in the wet and cold to cheer their teams.

The economy was not great, how could it be when vast fortunes has been spent on the war effort, but people were prepared to pay out from their meagre pay packets in the hope of finding some Saturday afternoon joy. The bitter winter season of 1947, the year the league proper was taking shape after the stop-gap war competitions, was the worst I can ever remember but the crowds continued to turn out and teams often attempted to play in farcical snow-bound conditions. The season went on until flaming June, Liverpool being handed the title when challengers Stoke lost 2 -1 at Sheffield United on 14 June 1947.

Anything was tried to keep games on, including marking lines on snow in red paint and taking braziers of burning "coke" fuel on to frozen pitches, but still about 150 matches were called off in three months. The war had blighted the career of a lot of stars although I saw at first hand how some like Joe Mercer had come through it and continued to play an excellent standard of football. Clubs that formed strong teams in 1939 found themselves having to build their teams again, because the wartime football was a pretty haphazard affair with all manner of guest players being used to make up sides, so there was little club stability.

The shortage of established players forced some clubs to try out their younger players and some of the early pre-war games were a little untidy but the crowds didn't seem to mind as they enjoyed life getting back to some sort of normality, although life was still pretty tough for millions of people.

To my mind, the war seemed to have had a bad effect on the Albion. In May 1939 they had finished third in Division III south and seemed to be, in the opinion of many people who followed them, on the "up." But eight years of desperate struggle later the picture was dismally different. In May 1947 they finished 17th and the era of the legendary Charlie Webb, who I had such respect for, came to an end. Former Albion hero Tommy Cook came in as manager and Charlie only stayed on until 1948 as general manager. Cook soon found himself under fire, and the papers were full of a pitch protest in November 1947 when they were third from bottom.

Cook's days were numbered, too, that month, and I had a job keeping up with the "goings-on" at the Goldstone. New manager Don Welsh joined in November 1947, fired up the team with some new signings, and only on goal difference failed to stop Albion finishing bottom in May 1948. So the talk of Sussex at the time was the indignity of Albion have to seek re-election to the League for the first time in their history, although no one seriously thought they would be thrown out of the League.

The remarkable thing I remember about that season was that despite Albion's poor showing the crowds went up and records were set several times as the national fever for football was reflected at the Goldstone Ground.

I remember that Charlie Webb, who was about 60 when he left, was always such a gentleman in a rough trade. On 28 September 1949 top teams Arsenal and Portsmouth came to the Goldstone for Charlie's testimonial and I ran a line. Charlie shook my hand before the kick-off and I felt emotional about it. There was a great deal of respect being paid to Charlie that day, but it was tinged with sadness because an astonishing era was passing that will never be repeated for however long Albion play. It was certainly a great honour for me to be there.

Charlie, a former Worthing player, had served the Albion as player and then manager and briefly as general manager from 1908 to 1948, becoming in his early 20s the first Albion player to win an international cap. Young, athletic, and handsome, he was one of Albion's first idols and it helped that he was a fine goal-getter, scoring a total of 79 goals in 275 matches. Although still an amateur, he scored the only goal as Southern league champions Albion beat mighty 1909-

1910 League champions Aston Villa 1-0 to win the FA Charity Shield, an astonishing result and their biggest honour to date, four years before the outbreak of World War One. Only injury halted his run of 64 Southern League goals in November 1914 and sadly it also ended his playing days. He then served in the First World War and ended his service in a most remarkable fashion.

Charlie must surely have been the only man in football history to be offered a manager's job while still a prisoner of war. The Germans caught him in France in March 1918 and while he was still in captivity the Albion wrote to him at the POW camp at and asked him to be manager, but it wasn't until Charlie was "demobbed" in June 1919 that he began his lifetime of work. He did much to keep Albion afloat in the dire Second World War days and I think Albion will always owe him a debt. Incidentally the talented Compton brothers, who both played top class cricket and football, were in the Arsenal line-up for that testimonial, but a young Portsmouth team rather surprisingly beat them 2-1.

I was sad to see Charlie eventually go. Don Welsh, who was pretty young for the job at 36, spent a few bob that maybe Charlie might have found useful in his time. I do not remember Welsh winning anything but he had an uphill task when he took over with Albion heading for the bottom. He was a good coach and the crowds went up, averaging just over 10,000 by the time he left. Liverpool took him in 1951 so they must have thought he had done some good work at the Goldstone.

Maybe Welsh laid the foundations for Billy Lane, who I got on OK with and who did well in his ten years. To this day my son Rod remembers what a nice bloke Billy was, having met him during his youth. One of my biggest disappointments was in season 1955-56, just as my top refereeing career was winding down, when attacking Albion scored an incredible 112 goals but still came second and missed promotion. Despite the near miss, it was one of

Albion's best seasons in their history with Albert Mundy banging in 28 league goals, Peter Harburn 27 in the League and Cup, and Denis Foreman hitting 15 in League and Cup. Crowds averaged 15,000, hitting 30,000 for the Leyton Orient game. I thought at the time, after years of watching the Albion at close quarters, that despite missing promotion this was the season when everyone believed Albion were finally moving on from their pre-war struggles into a new era, as if they had grown up as a club. But some of my pals thought maybe they had missed the boat, because football success is so fickle.

Billy stuck with it and got them up into the Second Division for the first time in 1958, by which time I had finished league refereeing. There was great rejoicing about their promotion among the Albion fans and indeed I think across Sussex because they have quite a wide fan base across the county, being the only full-time professional club. There must be many older Albion who remember young Adrian Thorne's hat-trick in four minutes that prompted the clinching 6-0 win against Watford before a record 31,038 League gate at the Goldstone. To think Thorne had only played a few games and only stepped in because Dave Sexton was injured.

I wasn't surprised that Billy got them up. In the earlier years he made some good signings and players like Eric Gill and Peter Harburn were very consistent, and I think Albert Mundy the centre-forward finished top scorer three seasons running, which some was going. Lane must have got the crowd interested pretty early on, because when I refereed a pre-season practice match at the Goldstone for the 1952-53 squad I was amazed to see afterwards the crowd was 7,000, which is about all they got for Nationwide Division One matches at their temporary home at Withdean Stadium last season, 2002-3, when sadly they got relegated from Division One to Division Two of the Nationwide League. In fairness that was their capacity at Withdean, a restriction that could be greatly hampering the club's finances. Albion have had a bit of a see-saw existence over the years, reaching Division One in 1979, when it was the top division of the league, and only losing the FA Cup final in 1983 to Manchester United after a replay. They have come desperately close to dropping out of the League, before climbing up again to Division One, this time in the new Nationwide League. At the moment they are near the top of Division Two and what a wonderful double it would be for them to go back up and get approval for that new stadium.

Thinking of Withdean, it was unbelievable that the club sold the famous Goldstone ground at the end of the 1990s and then had to share with Gillingham before camping out at Withdean. When you think about it, it's a fiasco that they have been without a proper ground of their own while other clubs, Southampton is one, have got their stadiums built. Their fans seem to have been amazingly loyal and deserve a lot better, and I hope the long delay does not hit their potential fan base when they do eventually get somewhere built, depending on planning inquiries and of course finding the finance.

Back in the 1950s things weren't quite such a struggle. The league crowds were up to about 20,000, maybe because Lane liked to play attacking football. In those days it cost the equivalent of about 10p to get in, but players were extremely poorly paid compared to what even the lowliest got in years to come. But in the refereeing world a few years before all this 50s success and just after the war I was still working my way up through Combination, Third Division, and FA Cup games towards the First Division games, while still turning out for local matches.

The newspapers had a field day when I created an unwanted piece of football history on 8 October 1949. I was back at The Den, as the fans called Millwall's ground, to referee Millwall against Crystal Palace. Being a local derby it was always going to be a needle match, and coming after the Millwall- Brighton game, where they had taken a dislike to me, I knew I was going to receive another hostile reception.

Supporters do not quickly forget. Right from the kick-off the boots were flying in and I can honestly say it was the hardest 45 minutes I've ever had to try to keep control of a game in England (I'd meet worse in South America later). As we went off at the interval the score was one-all, the talented former Arsenal player Ronnie Rooke having scored for Palace with a free kick that would have made Manchester United's former hero David Beckham, now with Real Madrid and probably the best free kick taker our football has ever seen, very proud.

But I had really had my fill of trouble and I told my linesmen: "Enough is enough – any more rough stuff and I'll start sending them off." We kicked off again and Rooke went thundering into the Millwall centre half and brought him clattering down. I beckoned to him and he walked away, turning his back on me. Then I suppose he had second thoughts, and turned around, walked back and started to give me a few choice words. Well, that was the final straw.

Without saying a word I pointed to the dressing room, indicating in the universal language of football: "You're off". Rooke blustered: "Oh no ref, you can't do that, I'm the Palace manager. You can't send me off,' and I really think he meant it. Rooke had been a magnificent bustling and powerful centre-forward for Arsenal with a shot like a rocket and when the Gunners won the league in 1947-48 he topped the League scorers list with 33 goals, making sure Arsenal led the season from beginning to end to win their sixth title in 11 seasons.

But the idol standing before me was just another player as far as the rules of the game were concerned. I made it crystal clear with a few sharp words that I could not have cared less if he'd been the Prime Minister, he was going off, and muttering darkly he turned on his heel and headed for the touchline. The dismissal had the desired effect and calmed the whole match down, making the second half very easy to handle and at full time, despite having played for 45 minutes with only 10 men Palace were the 3-2 winners.

As if losing a derby match was not bad enough, the supporters knew all too well that the result also removed any hope that Millwall had of gaining promotion into Division 2 that year. And so, once more, I am afraid I was not the favourite son of the home crowd as their rain of abuse showered on me as I left the pitch. After any sending-off the Football Association required the guilty player to appear before a commission where the incident that led to the dismissal would be examined and a further punishment could, if thought necessary, be handed out.

As usual, the hearing took place at the Great Western Hotel in London a few days after the match and Ronnie Rooke came up before the three men of the FA commission. It was a unique commission because it was the first time that a manager had ever been sent off and the members of the panel were clearly unsure how to handle the matter. After a long delay Ronnie was suspended for 14 days and told to pay the expenses of the commission, which was the usual procedure then.

He was allowed to pursue his duties as manager but his club was told he could not be paid for those two weeks of his playing suspension. At the hearing the chairman of Crystal Palace spoke in defence of his player-manager but he really did not help Ronnie's case when he told the panel that he thought "Mr Tarratt handled the game quite well under the circumstances." I think poor old Ronnie gave up any thought of getting off with a warning once he heard his chairman's words.

Since then I have met Ronnie on and off over the years in a variety of different circumstances. I recall Ronnie was at Hayward Heath Football Club for a time where he did some coaching - he coached in Horsham too and we met on several occasions, and we have exchanged cards at Christmas. The press reported at the time that I had called Rooke three times before I sent him off, and that Rooke claimed he was "mystified" by the decision.

The media made a big meal of this sending off proclaiming in big banner headlines that this was the first time in the league's history a player-manager had been sent off. It was a huge story and was given the sort of coverage Real Madrid's David Beckham gets nowadays (though Beckham gets it just for breathing sometimes). Rooke had notched himself a place in football history in another astonishing way as a young player for Fulham in the 1938-39 season, when he scored all six of Fulham's goals in a 6-0 FA Cup win against Bury, creating a record before the war blunted the impact of his career for many years until that sensational season with Arsenal.

The fuss that Rooke's dismissal by me caused all got lost in the mists of time over the years, as everything does eventually, but it was considered an extremely big deal then as the headlines showed and it sticks in my mind to this day. I handled the return match that Palace won 1-0 in front of 30,000 excited fans but there was no trouble at all from Rooke or anyone else.

I suspect there were not many Millwall fans thinking kind thoughts about me fifty years ago when they heard I was coming to Cold Blow Lane, as the Den's address was known before they moved much later to a new stadium. The tough no-nonsense dockers with their ripe and blunt language and the intimidating stadium gave the Millwall crowd a hard edge, and both referees and visiting teams needed a bit of bottle to take some of the verbal hammer they dished out.

I had seen plenty of the Albion, as I have said before, and it was a case of 'Oh no! Not him again!' when Millwall met Brighton and Hove Albion, on 3 October 1953 in Division Three South. All referees used to look forward to having the next month's list coming through the door. It detailed the matches we would be handling and told us who our linesmen were to be. Clearly some games were favourite fixtures that we all hoped to get, but for other matches I would have my fingers and toes crossed in the hope that they would not appear on my list.

Well, I was really horrified when I saw I had been appointed to referee Brighton away at Millwall. 'The Goldstone', Brighton's home ground in those days, had been my training place for several years – including when Charlie Webb and Bill Lane were in management, and all the players there were pals. Refereeing them would certainly put me on the spot so I rang the Football League headquarters in Preston and spoke to the legendary Alan Hardaker, then assistant secretary of the League, who went on to become League secretary from 1957 to 1977, after first joining them in 1947.

I explained the situation, thinking that he would swap me to another fixture. To my surprise nothing of the kind happened. "No, Mr Tarratt," Hardaker said, "It will be a good test for you, in fact I can tell you now that you're going to be assessed on that game so go ahead with the appointment." I was horrified but of course I had no choice in the matter. In those days referees were regularly assessed by selected representatives from the Football League, to make sure they were doing an adequate job and I reckoned I was in for a very hard time.

Not only would I have the notorious supporters at 'The Den' on my back but now I knew my every move would be watched by the beady eyes of an assessor. Life seems very hard on occasions. On the day of the match two friends accompanied me, one was an old pal, Fred Kempshal a director of Rice Brothers, the car people in Horsham, and the other was Arthur Barker, Superintendent of Horsham Police.

I knew Arthur quite well because he often came to my games – in fact I think he was football mad. Incidentally, he was the man who turned Horsham inside out and upside down by bringing in a one-way traffic system that caused complete havoc for many months. Despite that upset he was very popular amongst the public and within the local police service.

During our journey Arthur told us he was due at the Police Ball that evening and so he was hoping we would get away from the Millwall ground quickly when the game was over. "I have to entertain a lot of top brass, "he said, "including the local councillors." There was no reason why we might be delayed of course but something told me all was not well. I really was not looking forward to the afternoon and imagined that anything and everything that could go wrong would go wrong.

We arrived at The Den, parked the car in the tunnel underneath the main stand, and I went off to the changing room. One linesman had arrived before me and was reading the match programme.

"Look at this Ralph", he said, and showed me the page that featured the Millwall chairman's remarks.

In very heavy black type it read: **"Today's referee is Mr. R.Tarratt who lives in Sussex a few miles from Hove, and he trains with the Brighton players twice a week."**

Well, you can imagine how I felt reading that. If I had had no concerns before about the job ahead those programme notes were a guarantee that the Millwall players and supporters were going to give me a rough ride. "Thank you Mr. Chairman" I thought as I walked out through the tunnel. I can still hear the greeting I received coming out onto the pitch and whenever I made any decision that favoured the visiting team the Millwall supporters went mad.

To rub it in for them Albion's goals were scored by two players who did not really feature regularly in the first team during their spells at the Goldstone. In fact, most people who can remember Tommy Bisset after all these years would probably remember him as a full-back.

The goal I noted he scored against Millwall that day was his only goal of the season and he only scored five in his 123 matches in ten years. But you can do anything with statistics, you know. The records show Bisset only played seven times at centre forward, which with five goals makes him probably the most consistent striker in Albion's history, which is one way of looking at things. Like I say, you can do what you like with figures.

Little Scot Jimmy Sirrell, probably better remembered as a manager, scored Albion's other goal. I remember him as being an intelligent player but sometimes a bit slow. He only stayed three seasons and for a midfield player his 17 goals in 58 matches was not a bad tally.

Also in that Albion line-up was Jimmy Langley, who had only been signed in July from Leeds when he was 24.

Seeing Langley flying down the wing and tackling like a demon I couldn't understand why Leeds, who had played him as a winger, ever let him go. He had the speed you would expect from a winger, but he had bags of skill and his fitness was pretty amazing. I think he missed about five matches in his stay with the Albion from 1953-57 and I suppose no one was shocked when Fulham bought him and he gave them great service, proving as popular at Craven Cottage as he was adored at the Goldstone.

That day at Cold Blow Lane he sat tight on the Millwall winger and also bombed up the line himself, but he took some stick from the disgruntled docker boys in the seething 21,000 crowd. After Bisset and Sirrell had dropped their bombshells and the game ended my linesmen and I retreated to our changing room after the final whistle. I had my bath, got dressed and met up again with Fred and Arthur.

The trouble really started as we set off back to my car. A large sergeant policeman stopped us at the gate, looked me firmly in the eye and said: "If you go out there sir I think you might not come back alive". There were literally hundreds of people outside the gates and they certainly did not look happy or friendly.

Superintendent Barker explained to the sergeant that it was absolutely imperative that he got back to Horsham very quickly and the sergeant suggested he talk to the Superintendent in charge at the ground. "But," he said, pointing to me, "I have to tell you sir that there's no way we're letting him through, and his car is staying where it is, beneath the stand."

To cut a long story short there did not seem much point in arguing the case and so we were stuck inside the ground for four and a half hours. We eventually got back to Horsham and rushed straight to the Drill Hall but Superintendent Barker was only just in time to say goodbye to his guests and as for his poor wife, well, she was in hysterics. I am not sure he ever forgave me for that day.

Another match in the 50s brought fear of imminent death to me but had nothing to do with events inside the ground. Having had two long car journeys to games during the week, I decided to use the luxury of the train to Nottingham for a game. When I arrived I had a call from a Nottingham referee, Reg Leafe, a great friend of mine, to say he would meet me off my train journey in his car and take me to the ground because his particular match was off.

After picking me up we were invited into the boardroom, which was the usual practice in those days. What a change in what the officials get today – they are never welcome in the boardroom or to anything except to have their bath and go. The game over, I had a quick bath, as my London train did not give me much time for a good 'natter'. Setting out for the car park, we were confronted by a large figure wearing a long coat.

He emerged from behind a bush, and we saw to our horror he was carrying a long knife. I had never experienced anything like it in my career but we did not hang around to dwell on the matter.

My pal Reg packed me into the car, we slammed the door and we dashed for the station.

We were of course glad to escape any potential danger but anyway we were short of time because if I missed the London train it would have meant a long wait at the station.

I was in too much of a hurry to get on the train to think about my close escape but once I took my seat I wondered just what this intruder might have had in mind for one or both of us.

I got my answer just before midnight when I received a call from Reg from Nottingham to say he had picked up a policeman at the station entrance, and the policeman had told Reg that they had caught the culprit before leaving the ground.

The man was arrested and taken into custody to appear in court the following Wednesday. As I had a cup replay that day I was unable to go up to hear the case, not that I really wanted to. It appears he was an out of work miner with a very unsavoury record but there was no evidence he intended to injure me. It just felt like he might at the time, I must say.

On the subject of Reg Leafe, I remember him to this day as the finest referee I ever came across and he must certainly be one of the best ever. Not only that, he was always immensely helpful and kind to me and I count myself lucky that our paths crossed in life. While I am remembering referees, long before our paths crossed in international circles Stanley Rous, later of course Sir Stanley was a top referee for eight years, officiating at 34 internationals and the 1934 Cup Final when Manchester City beat Portsmouth 2-1.

As I got involved in the organisation of local refereeing as well as my top-flight duties on the pitch I appreciated how that background of Sir Stanley helped him understand the needs of the game, when he became a superb administrator with the FA and later with FIFA. On a local level he will be remembered by older people in Haywards Heath for performing the opening ceremony before about 5,000 people for the splendid new Hanbury Park Stadium in Haywards Heath in 1952, when Horsham did the honours as visitors. That was typical of him, to lend his support to a local team because he loved the game of football.

Ralph's birthplace at Cox Farm, Warnham

Ralph relaxes with father Ernest and brother Basil

Linesman-referee stood 'no nonsense'

SHIN-GUARDS for referees would probably find one supporter in Mr. S. E. Law, of West Bromwich. In a collision with Doug. Lishman at Highbury he accidentally got a boot scraped down his leg and it all but put him out of the game (writes **GEORGE CHISHOLM**).

He hobbled about for 23 minutes and then exchanged duties with linesman R. E. Tarratt, of Horsham, for the last hour.

Some players were inclined to be argumentative with Mr. Tarratt, with vocal support from parts of the crowd — seeing Manchester United deservedly end Arsenal's unbeaten home record—but he made it understood that he would not stand for any nonsense, and maintained praiseworthy control.

After 23 minutes of much hobbling, Mr. Laws decides to send himself off and (below) he changes places with Mr. R. E. Tarratt, one of the linesmen.

Newspapers report Ralph's surprise 1951 Arsenal - Manchester United debut

Ralph with first wife Billie at the christening of daughter Sonia 1936

RONNIE ROOKE BANNED 14 DAYS

RONNIE ROOKE, Crystal Palace player-manager, was yesterday suspended by the Football Association for 14 days from Monday.

An FA official said that the suspension did not affect Rooke's position as manager, but he could not draw any salary as a player during his term of suspension.

Rooke (pictured alongside) was sent off the field during the Millwall v. Crystal Palace match on October 8, and asked for a personal hearing of his case by a Commission yesterday.

He was ordered to pay the costs of the inquiry.

In the statement the Commission regretted having to take disciplinary action against a player-manager, who, they said, "because of his added responsibility, is expected to exercise greater care that his actions, both on and off the field of play, are not likely to bring the game into disrepute."

This Makes (Legal) Football History

By Sunday Dispatch Reporter

PLAYER-MANAGER, captain and centre forward of Crystal Palace, Ronnie Rooke was sent off the field by the referee, Mr. R. E. Tarratt, of Sussex, shortly before the end of the match between Crystal Palace and Millwall at The Den yesterday.

Never before has a player-manager been ordered from the field during a game.

In any case of misdemeanour on the field the referee's report is sent to the FA. They consider the circumstances and order the offender to report before them. After reviewing the evidence they have the power to administer punishment, ranging from a reprimand to suspension.

Suspension for a professional brings with it loss of pay.

Manager—Unpaid

The position of a player-manager who is suspended has never previously had to be considered. Should such an event take place, what is his position?

If he is suspended as a player, does it automatically follow that he is suspended as a manager?

Consensus of opinion last night was that it does. Since a player-manager is entitled to be paid only the maximum wage allowed to players (£12 per week), he is in fact not paid for his managerial duties.

Should he be allowed to pursue them unpaid?

Services Lost

Under Rule 45 of the F.A. any member, player, official, or spectator found guilty of violations or misconduct is liable to suspension; and while suspended "shall not be allowed to take part in football or football management. . . ."

This would seem to indicate that if a player-manager is sent off the field in his capacity as a player, the club lose his services not only on the field but off the field, in his executive duties, while the suspension lasts.

Press reports of historic Rooke dismissal at The Den 1949

Ralph (2nd from left) and Ronnie Rooke (far right) at FA Commission 1949

Ralph and 69,000 watch Charlton keeper Bartram v Arsenal - The Valley 1951

Brighton Boys v Redhill and Reigate English Schools Trophy replay The Goldstone November 1946

Ralph checks broken net Gillingham 1947 (Chatham News)

Taking the field Chile v Spain Santiago July 1953

Lining up Portugal v Argentina Lisbon 1952

A 163,000 crowd greets Ralph at Argentina v Spain July 1953. Inset: Ralph leaves Heathrow with officials for South America

Which way? Ralph at kick-off at Fratton Park, Portsmouth. (Evening News Portsmouth)

Albion v Nancy (France) FA Jubilee match Goldstone 1951

Too cold to stay?

by KEN SMITH

BRENTFORD 1   **WEST HAM UTD.** ... 1
(abandoned at half-time)

SIX THOUSAND disappointed supporters did not take kindly to Referee R. E. Tarrat's decision to abandon this game at half-time with the score at one each.

A strong police contingent were on duty outside the referee's entrance but the crowd filed quietly away.

Referee Tarrat decided, after consultation with the linesmen that the touchlines were indistinguishable owing to the snow which had fallen steadily throughout the entire half.

West Ham centre - forward, Maroney, normally a wing half back, had given the visitors the lead with a fine drive in the 22nd minute. Thirteen minutes later, Brentford inside-right, Bowie, was brought down and right-back Monk equalised from the spot.

ARSENAL F.C. OFFICIAL PROGRAMME

COLOURS—SHIRTS: RED, WHITE SLEEVES AND COLLARS. KNICKERS: WHITE. STOCKINGS: BLUE, WHITE RINGS, WHITE TOPS.

ARSENAL

Swindin
Goal

2 Barnes — Right Back   **3 Smith, L.** — Left Back

4 Forbes — Right Half   **5 Daniel** — Centre Half   **6 Mercer** — Left Half (Capt.)

7 Milton — Outside Right   **8 Logie** — Inside Right   **9 Holton** — Centre Forward   **10 Lishman** — Inside Left   **11 Roper** — Outside Left

Referee
Mr. S. E. Law
(West Bromwich)

Linesmen
Mr. R. E. Tarratt (Horsham) — Red Flag
Mr. E. P. Haynes (Godalming) — Yellow Flag

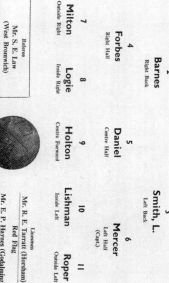

Result of corresponding match last season—Arsenal 3, Manchester United 0.

11 Bond — Outside Left   **10 Downie** — Inside Left   **9 Rowley** — Centre Forward   **8 Pearson** — Inside Right   **7 Berry** — Outside Right

6 Cockburn — Left Half   **5 Chilton** — Centre Half   **4 Carey** — Right Half (Capt.)

3 Byrne — Left Back   **2 McNulty** — Right Back

Crompton
Goal

MANCHESTER UNITED

COLOURS—SHIRTS: RED. KNICKERS: WHITE. STOCKINGS: RED AND WHITE TOPS.
Owing to clash of colours Manchester United will today wear blue shirts.

9

Reminders from Ralph's extensive scrapbooks

Ralph jokes with "Fat" Fred Emney at Goldstone Ground Hove c.1956 (Evening Argus)

Referee's Wife: "I've come with him this time."

Favourite cartoons from Ralph's collection

Air Raid Warnings

IN THE EVENT OF AN AIR RAID

All Exits from the Ground
WILL BE OPENED

so that those who wish can leave as speedily and as quietly as possible.

COVER IS PROVIDED UNDER THE STAND
for those who wish to remain.

THE NEAREST PUBLIC SHELTERS
are at the
RECREATION GROUND FULHAM PALACE ROAD
via any of the Streets opposite the Exits of the Ground.

As accommodation at the Public Shelter is limited we advise all who can to obtain shelter elsewhere.

No money can be refunded or re-admittance tickets issued when a match has been abandoned on account of an Air Raid.

The Management request that patrons will at all times distribute themselves about the ground and banks as much as possible to avoid crowding. Please remember that in the event of an emergency you will greatly assist by keeping calm.

"Those who wish can leave"- Air Raid warning Fulham v Notts Forest 18th May 1940

Ralph in Cairo with pal c.1943

Ralph's programme for Chile v Spain July 1953 Santiago

Ralph and team at Anfield for Liverpool v Everton in the 1950's

Ralph's second wife Edith with Ralph and son Rod

Ralph with newly graduated daughter Kim

Rod wins Sussex Champion of Champions bar billiards title 1970-71

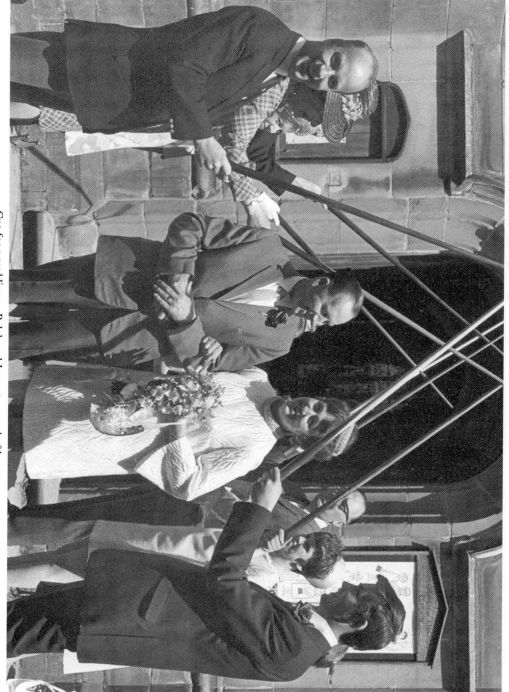

Cue for a wedding as Ralph and Joy get a guard of honour

Ralph and guests at the Ralph Tarratt Charity Sports Dinner he organised at Southwater Cricket Club in March 2003, standing left to right Frank King, David Ball, Alan Needham, Mohammed Khan. Seated are Ralph and guest speaker Chris Adams, skipper of the 2003 county champions Sussex. (County Times)

Ralph at his charity dinner in March 2003 with Chris Adams, skipper of 2003 county champions Sussex

The cricket picture Ralph waited a liftime for. Skipper Chris Adams and team celebrate the first county championship title for Sussex on 18th September 2003 at the County Ground, Hove. (courtesy Steven Dennett)

Later in the book I will tell you how I came across Mr Rous again at the peak of my own career, but I certainly think he is one of our great names of football, on or off the pitch. You'd need a book to tell about his contribution to the game, but of special interest to me were the courses he developed for referees, which eventually filtered through to local football circles, He also re-wrote the laws of the game, which a lot of us thought had needed doing for some time to avoid muddle, but he had to fight a bit to get it done. It was one of the great privileges of my long life to have met such a great football man.

I think that among the modern-day referees Allan Gunn, who combined his refereeing with work for a Burgess Hill firm, was one of my favourites to see in action. I liked his style, he was obviously lean and extremely fit, as any referee needs to be, so he was nearly always in the right place at the right time, and he had a great personal presence about him on the pitch. Like Reg Leafe, Allan had authority, but he tempered it with a common-sense attitude and it looked as if he got on well with players, which shouldn't be surprising because he had played County League football with Whitehawk before taking up the whistle.

Like my pal Reg, he got to referee an FA Cup Final and both of them richly deserved it. When I read in the Evening Argus a few years back that Alan had refereed a primary school match in the run up to his FA Cup final match I wasn't surprised. He always seemed confident but not a big head and liked to promote football at a local level. He was such a brilliant referee in every way. He had a good rapport with players, that was his strength. I like to think I had a little of that too, because it certainly helps. It makes a hell of a difference.

I used it to my advantage in the late 40s and 50s to strike a rapport with Albion. When the managers at Brighton arranged a charity match, they might be playing a foreign team like Hamburg, or perhaps a testimonial for a loyal and consistent player like Jess Willard, I would often do the game. Also I was able to appoint my own linesmen, so it also had a spin-off for local Sussex referees as it gave them the chance to run the line in front of a bigger crowd than usual. So I hope I was some help in getting them more experience.

I needed all the experience I could muster sometimes in some unusual situations, some of them dictated by extreme weather. Like the time I played King Canute and the Thames played the part of the disobedient "sea" while an impatient crowd waited. More than half a century has passed since I had that strange sensation of waiting for the Thames to recede to start a match, along with about 30,000 people, but I can still recall the worried look of some Fulham officials as Old Father Thames threatened their big match which I think was in September 1949.

I had driven myself and arrived at Craven Cottage in excellent time but at the ground a rather worried looking official greeted me. He asked me to the chairman's office straight away but would not explain why I was being summoned. Well, before I could even get out of my car I saw Tommy Trinder, the chairman, coming towards me. He was a comedian of the old school who had grown up in music hall and was loved by many as a talented performer.

Everyone in football recognised his passion for the game and for Fulham Football Club in particular. Mr Trinder greeted me politely and said: "Hello Mr Tarratt, I've got a problem." He went on to explain that earlier the superintendent of police had requested that the gates open early because the whole area around Fulham was clogged with the traffic coming to the game. Visitors Newcastle have always been known as fanatical supporters and true to form they were piling down to London in their cars and coaches, and also on trains.

The police had told Mr Trinder that the roads were entirely full up and so in an effort to help the chairman had offered to open the gates of the ground early and let the fans in. Looking very worried, he said to me: "I have a horrible feeling I might have been wrong." Certainly at that time I could not see a problem. My officials and I would get changed and we could expect an exciting afternoon. But what I did not know was what was waiting for me on the pitch.

The Fulham ground sat right alongside the south bank of the River Thames and soon, with a very high tide, there was a good inch and a half of river covering the whole pitch. It only took a moment of inspection to realise things were not too good, in fact I thought we would be lucky to get a game on. From talking with the Fulham groundsman I learned that the river could in fact recede very quickly, that flooding was a regular occurrence and that, in his opinion, there was a good chance that the turf would dry quite quickly once the tide went out.

So, on the strength of what the groundsman advised, the linesmen and I went back to our dressing room after telling the ground staff that we would wait for a while and inspect again in half an hour. We had no sooner sat down than Mr Trinder rushed in. "Look Mr Tarratt," he said, "it is still possible, I think it has gone down a bit. If it is still possible to get the game under way, will you do so? I would be very grateful and with a ground full of impatient fans it might get us out of a bit of trouble."

I told Mr Trinder what I had already told his staff: "I'll make another inspection quite soon. We have plenty of time before our scheduled 3pm kick off and from what I've been told there's every chance we'll get the game away on time." He was quiet for a moment before he said: "I'll tell you what I'll do. I've got a friend of mine running in a pantomime in London. If you and your linesmen would like to come up we'll give you a box one evening – how about that?" '

"Fair enough", I told him, "but that doesn't change a thing. I'll inspect the ground just before kick off as I've already told you." Well, I waited but at five minutes to three the water had not gone down at all. Mr Trinder seemed very surprised. "I'll bet there's not another game off in London" he said, which hardly seemed a surprise to me. "Which other London ground has to cope with the tide?" I asked him, but by now he could only accept that we would not be playing football at Craven Cottage that afternoon.

In the end, to everyone's relief, the crowd went home with a better spirit than might have been expected and the match was played a few days later, when the ground was in perfect condition. Fulham won two goals to one with goals by Rob Thomas and Bedford Jezzard, it was good game in front of 39,000 people, and everybody but the visiting fans, who always hate losing, was happy.

Mr Trinder was not at the game, but up in London at a show, I believe. He did send a message to say that my linesmen and I were still welcome to come to the pantomime. I didn't go but I gather one of my linesmen, a chap from Reading who had rather a large family, took the opportunity, went up there had a wonderful evening and they even went behind scenes after the show, had drinks and met the cast.

So really, it all ended well. Looking back it seems an absurd situation and with hindsight after so long it seems Fulham had only themselves to blame. They knew better than anyone how the state of the river might affect their ground and that playing the game that day was unlikely. But once they had let the fans into the ground they had a problem on their hands. I only lived about 30 miles from London and why they did not call me in early I really cannot understand. It could have turned out very badly and I think Fulham realised that they had made mistakes.

In the end, it all ended fairly happily though, as every good pantomime should. Trinder had a remarkable record, chairing Fulham from 1945 to 1977, and I recall this unusual meeting with him with fond memories after so many years.

It was not just at professional level that I had problems with waterlogged grounds. When I arrived to referee the Bognor and Haywards Heath Sussex County league match in the 50s we had to delay the kick off nearly an hour while people mopped about an inch of water off the pitch. Even then, it was so bad that we narrowed the pitch to avoid the worst areas and had to re-mark the lines. I can't imagine such a thing happening nowadays at County League level, but it showed how keen people were to play.

The amazing efforts of the gang of volunteers were rewarded with a cracking 3-3 draw before about 400 people which the media called "laughter-raising" and "thrilling" as the ball stuck when players thought it would roll, but we got through. The problems had been caused by a fierce storm the night before and a morning of rain. For Heath, who fielded seven reserves, it was a little bit of history for them. It was their last match before joining the Metropolitan League, which had teams like West Ham and Arsenal A teams in it, and among their scorers was Cyril Hodges, later to become a great favourite of the Goldstone crowd as trainer to Brighton and Hove Albion.

Unexpected problems caused by the elements and human error always seemed to surface both at junior and senior football level. A hole in the net, more rain, and a mistake by linesmen in another match in 1947 nearly had me in a lot of trouble. I recall it was a game between Gillingham v Northampton Town and it was played during a violent thunder storm which broke over our heads as we ran on to inspect the pitch.

Play had been going for about 10 minutes when I awarded Gillingham a free kick and the ball finished up in the back of the net. As I blew for a goal and pointed to the centre-spot I heard the Northampton goalkeeper shouting at me and gesturing toward a gaping hole at the side of the net near the post. Seeing this I realised that it was quite impossible to decide whether it had been a goal or not. I ran over to my linesman on the goal line but he couldn't confirm which way the ball had entered the net – either in through the goal or in via the hole in the side.

Given the uncertainty I had to rule out a score and so no goal was awarded. Well, the Gillingham fans were disgusted of course, and they let me know all too clearly what they thought of my decision in no uncertain terms. Before restarting play I examined both nets very carefully and to my horror they were absolutely falling to pieces. I ordered that new nets must be fitted which was greeted with a mixture of bemusement, amusement, and annoyance by the crowd of about 11,000.

But somehow they found some nets from somewhere. After a long delay the match went ahead with new nets on both goals and Gillingham won, which at least kept most people happy. Of course there was an enquiry afterwards and the Football League fined the club. Gillingham in turn sacked the groundsman responsible as the nets were found to be last season's, and they should have been discarded.

And sadly both the linesmen were taken off the Football League's list, which seemed harsh as I knew them to be very capable. But it is always the linesmen's first duty on coming on to the pitch to examine the nets before the match kicks off and clearly they had failed to do so on this occasion. Perhaps they had an excuse, given that that awful storm, but it certainly reminds me that in those days any mistakes were firmly punished by the authorities.

I mentioned earlier in the book the terrible winter of 1947 when the crowds still turned out despite blizzards and snowdrifts. Five years later, on 29 March 1952, a date I know precisely because I kept the programme and the press cuttings, the snow got me into a spot of bother with the Brentford crowd but also gave me a funny memory of the match.

There was a carpet of snow about three inches thick on the pitch but I thought it was safe enough to make a start. That may sound strange now, but that is how things were half a century ago. No one had under-soil pitch heating and the league programme had to go ahead if at all possible, if the pitch was considered safe for players.

Visitors West Ham obviously had others ideas about the possibility of play, and had not even bothered to make their usual prompt start from their meeting place to the match, believing they would not be having a game. It was not until they got a call saying the match was still on that they made a late dash to the ground. Inside their coach weaving their way through the traffic the players were stripping off and ran into the ground wearing their kit under coats, a pretty farcical scene but in its way very funny.

The comedy did not quite end there. A blizzard soon began to make conditions worse but Brentford winger Johnny Paton decided to put a bit of humour into the proceedings after I awarded a corner to the Bees, as Brentford have always been known. Paton carefully and with great craft built a large pyramid of snow to act as a sort of golf "tee" for the ball, to laughs from the crowd. Paton might have been playing to the crowd a bit and a newspaper recalled that this was "not exactly to referee Tarratt's liking."

Technically, perhaps, Paton was in the wrong but I did enjoy the funny side of it and chuckled to myself. All the newspapers later picked up this little story and widely publicised it. As the game progressed I wondered just how we might complete this match because conditions were worsening by the minute and the lines were becoming fainter under a blanket of snow. We had even more fun when I awarded a penalty to Brentford.

By now the penalty spot had disappeared and the decent-sized crowd of 5,900 perishing souls shivered in amazement as the players joined me searching for the penalty spot like some kind of sunken treasure. When we eventually found it Freddy Monk promptly scored from the penalty for Bees, but by half-time, with the score 1-1, I decided that enough was enough.

A rather upset crowd of supporters, to put it mildly, gathered near the ground offices to protest at the decision, but, as was reported later in the press, I explained it was impossible to keep the lines clear of snow. The supporters were steamed up despite the shivering cold but they eventually dispersed although not without some choice insults in my direction.

There were a couple of big names playing in that bizarre match, although with the ball stopping in the snow no-one had much chance to distinguish themselves, however good they were.

The biggest star of all on the pitch that day was Tommy Lawton, who dominated English football from the 30s to the 50s as one of the most complete centre forwards ever to grace a football pitch. He was as big a name as anyone playing in today's football and the Bees had somehow managed to sign him from Notts County despite their relatively lowly position in the football world.

Lawton had already drawn a massive 30,000 crowd for his first match for the Bees, and I remember the sensation of the whole thing featuring on the newsreels. Football stories didn't come any bigger. If you had seen as I did the appalling weather leading up to that game I refereed when Lawton played his second game at Griffin Park you'd marvel that his name drew nearly 6,000 people through the biting wind, snow, and icy roads to the game.

It didn't make it any easier when I came to abandoning the match because I knew how much effort everyone had made, but things were becoming a farce and might have become dangerous. Even in those conditions you could see Lawton was still brave, quick, strong, skilful, and probably the finest header of a ball in a forward line that there has been. Believe me, when he rose to head a ball he seemed to hover like a helicopter above the turf and then punch the heavy ball with huge power with his forehead like a punchbag.

No player nowadays heads like Lawton. Young Tommy Taylor, who died in the Munich air crash, might have been as good if he had lived to reach his peak, but I cannot think of a modern-day player like him, perhaps Van Nistelrooy the Dutch Manchester United striker, who from what I have seen on television has his pace, skill, and courage, but isn't nearly as good in the air.

No wonder about five years before Notts County had shelled out a record British transfer fee of £20,000 to buy Lawton, then 28, from First Division Chelsea in 1947. It created a sensation because County were only in the Third Division. Lawton's appearance for County against the Albion in April 1948, when he was England's centre-forward, drew a record Goldstone gate of 19,572 and he scored twice in a 3-1 win as Albion headed for bottom place despite the biggest crowds in their history so far.

Five years later it might have been thought by the more sceptical among the Bees supporters on that snow-bound day at Griffin Park in 1952 that Lawton was past his best at 33 after leaving behind Everton, Chelsea, and Notts County.

In fact he didn't stay long at Brentford, who were in the Second Division and had paid a record club fee of £16,000 for him. He wasn't much of a success as player-manager there but he still had plenty left in the tank and in 1953 he went up a class as a player and signed for Arsenal in Division One. He had three excellent years at Highbury in a colourful autumn to his first class career despite being 34.

When I turned up for the West Ham match Lawton had only signed for Brentford two weeks before, and the place was buzzing with Lawton fever, but he didn't bring them great success on the pitch. His legends lived on, though. The Charlton goalkeeper Sam Bartram, who I often came across in my refereeing travels and who became a friend as I will expand upon later, often told the story of how in one game he was watching a flighted cross while Lawton launched himself into the air to meet it. Lawton had an uncanny knack of timing his jump so well that he hung like a hawk above defenders and this gave him a precious split second start on them.

Bartram said that on this occasion Lawton shouted: "Top left hand corner, Barty" and according to Bartram, who should know, that is where the ball went. In that snow-bound game at Brentford I was refereeing, Lawton had little chance to show the immense talent that scored a hat-trick at 17 for Burnley against Tottenham. I suppose as a youngster he was the equivalent of the present boy wonder Wayne Rooney, from Everton, who looks very good but has a long way to go.

The fact that within a year of that hat-trick for Burnley Everton paid £6,500 for young Lawton to succeed the majestic Dixie Dean spoke volumes for his ability, and he helped them win the league and played for England. After joining Chelsea he stayed only one full season before he was involved in that remarkable transfer to Notts County. Although County were languishing in the Third Division they got back that record £20,000 fee when crowds went up from 10,000 to about 30,000.

That freezing day in 1952 it was an honour to share the pitch, albeit too briefly, with man who scored 231 goals in 390 league games and 22 in 23 games for England. As a footnote to that Brentford game I see in the programme, which I have kept, that the departure of a certain Jimmy Hill from Brentford to Fulham is noted. Jimmy, a strong minded individual, who lives at Hurstpierpoint, near Burgess Hill, later became a players champion as chairman of the Professional Footballers Association, and I think literally changed the fortunes of players in the 1960s by getting the maximum wage abolished.

It's incredible to think that top players up to then could earn no more than £20 a week, dropping to £17 in the summer. How sad that it all came too late for players like Tommy Lawton and Stanley Matthews at their peak, who although well paid compared with ordinary workers, were certainly not adequately recompensed for the huge crowds they attracted. Crowds forget that when some of these stars got injured and were literally kicked out of the game a lot of them ran into desperate money troubles.

Now top players like Ryan Giggs and David Beckham can play free from financial worries from their late 20s or early 30s if they look after their money, although they have to live with the social restrictions being a top player entails nowadays. I don't think football ever becomes just a hobby because they are rich. It might apply to some I suppose, but I still think a lot of them love playing in front of huge crowds, as I loved refereeing in front of them.

I think most players are still driven by their ambition to win trophies and their professionalism. Certainly lower down the league players have never made a fortune, but in my experience for all the hard knocks players got most players simply loved playing. What a strange fascination football is.

Seeing Jimmy Hill on the television as a commentator for the BBC over the years, he now works for Sky, I think people forget that he was a successful football manager with Coventry, taking them from the Third to the First Division, and a top class club director, so he has been through every level of football. I haven't always agreed with what Jimmy said, but since he has seen the game from both sides of the fence I have always respected his opinion and I have come across him in the many kind works he does for charity, quite a lot of which does not get publicised.

A trip to the excellent ground at Ipswich was one that I and my colleagues and indeed players always looked forward to making and one game towards the end of my first-class career still has great personal happy memories for me. The playing surface at the Ipswich ground was always 100% - their secret, I think was a special local turf laid on a deep ledger of clinkers enabling the water to drain away very quickly. They had the reputation of never having a game postponed for drainage troubles.

Their groundsman once told me he thought the clinkers came from a local brewery – Cobbolds – the Suffolk brewery. John Cobbold was the chairman of Ipswich Town then and the whole family were keen supporters of the club. I do not remember the game itself being particularly remarkable and it ended 0-1 in favour of the visitors on that day in September 1955.

However, reflecting now over the years, that day has become very important to me. Several years after the game I picked up the telephone at home and heard a tiny, hesitant voice ask: "Is that you Dad?" It was my daughter, Sonia, whom I had not seen for many years. We had lost touch after her mother Billie and I had divorced in 1947 and I often wondered how she was, hoping she was well and happy. When the divorce was finalised Sonia was in boarding school but I did not know where. Now the years had gone by, she had moved to Ipswich, and was married with two children.

Sonia said that by chance her husband-to-be was at that Ipswich match. This was a rare occasion as he managed a local side in the Ipswich League who usually played on a Saturday. On that particular day they had no fixture and he'd gone to Portman Road. He had mentioned after the game that my name was in the programme. Taking a chance that the referee and her long-lost dad were one and the same she contacted the Ipswich Town club.

Very reluctantly they put her through to their manager Alf Ramsey, a man I had come across years before as a player and whom I greatly admired as a player's manager but someone who was well known to take a very distant view about us officials. He was a very offhanded kind of chap, but I think a brilliant manager, which was proved by his work 11 years later winning the World Cup for England at Wembley.

But Sonia got the telephone number she wanted. After so long apart it took Sonia many years to actually telephone me, but hearing her voice that Friday evening when she did was a wonderful thrill.

One incident from the game that day is still recalled by the Ipswich club historian, although it seems to have slipped my memory. Lining up for the re-start after half-time I blew my whistle and play began.

Apparently, I had not noticed that a tea lady was heading across the pitch to get back to the kitchens, oblivious to the game now going on around her. I stopped the match and players and crowd gave her a rousing cheer as she made her way back beneath the stands. It is impossible to remember all the funny little moments that happened along the way of course, although all the cuttings I kept help me recall most of them. It was Sonia who recalled 'the tale of the tea lady' after hearing about it herself. I was glad we made contact again and were only a telephone call away.

Incidentally the return match in January 1956 was one of my last league matches, and by then Ipswich was top of the division and not far behind them was my home county club Brighton. Sonia, who is a football fan, has some recollections of her own for this book about the occasional problems when she watched me referee. She said: "I can recall going to one game when I was quite young and standing with the press. I was suppose I was eight or nine. I remember dad being booed off the field and people throwing bad tomatoes at my dad and wondering why they should be so mean and unfair."

It wasn't all abuse. I also had a few laughs. One of the strangest requests I had was to take part in a press call with some Albion players at the Goldstone in the mid-50s. When I got there I was greeted by the larger-than-life and extremely amiable comedian Fred Emney, known fondly in the 50s and 60s as The Fat Man with the Cigar, who later appeared in the hit film The Italian job with Michael Caine. The Evening Argus, well known in Sussex for its extensive coverage of the fluctuating fortunes of the Albion over the years, was there to capture the moment in a lovely photograph that still makes me smile today. Unfortunately, Fred later tripped during a filming session, broke a leg, and the filming was never completed. He went to the Royal Sussex County Hospital in Brighton.

By the mid-Fifties my top Football league career was nearing its end but I was still coming across some big names. In November 1955 I handled the Swansea-Liverpool Division Two match. Liverpool had the wonderful Billy Liddell and a player who became key figure at Anfield, Ronnie Moran, and Swansea, who were top after 15 matches, had a great quartet in Len and Ivor Allchurch, Cliff Jones, and Mel Charles.

Maybe few people remember these players nowadays, but take it from me they were more than a match for anyone playing today. I agree the game is much faster and generally the players are probably fitter, but those marvellous players like Liddell would have looked good in any company.

Cliff Jones, of course, who I recall was quick and a great crosser of the ball, would go on to be part of that wonderful "push and run" Tottenham team who did the League and Cup Double in 1961. Jones differed from modern players in that he went behind the full-backs and pulled the ball back from the by-line, which made it much easier for the likes of Bobby Smith to score from his crosses. Nowadays few players have the speed or skill to do that.

Away from the relative glamour of Football League clubs, the local clubs often gave me great hospitality and none more than a visit to a Sussex club. The great comedy actor Norman Wisdom was once president of West Chiltington Football Club and as chairman of the Horsham Association, I attended their annual dinner. They had won their league and Norman gave them a night to remember. He must have played every instrument imaginable to entertain the crowd.

Eventually my wife and I left and we got home in the very early hours, and Norman was apparently still in full song. When he was on the Board at Brighton and Hove Albion Football Club in the 60s, which helped raise their profile, he was a great help to me in introducing me to some of the right people.

As business and refereeing blossomed I gained a new honour as my time for bowing out of top class refereeing because of upper age restrictions approached in 1955.

My selection as referee for an important amateur international on 12 November 1955 between England and Germany at Tottenham Hotspur's ground at White Hart Lane was a great honour for me, and I still have the plaque they gave me. Amateur football had a much bigger following in those days and it was great experience for me to referee before an excited crowd of 15,000. Make no mistake this level of football was taken seriously especially at international standard.

I certainly had plenty of goals to note down, with Germany winning 3-2. It is interesting to recall that the gate receipts were £1,043, which was a fair amount of money in those days. Afterwards I joined the teams for a dinner at White's Hotel in Lancaster Gate, London. The menu, which I have kept, was cantaloupe frappe, supreme de Sole Bon-Vivieur, Tournedos Sauté Marechale, Boutons de Bruzelles, Pommes Macaire, Parfait Glace Seville aux Comice Rosaria, and Gaufrettes, with Canapes des Gourmets. Quite a mouthful one way or the other but the match was significant for me in that being chosen for international duty was some recognition of the time I had spent improving myself as a referee, although I have to say every minute of it was time in my long life that I enjoyed spending.

In the next chapter I will recall one of the greatest moments in my refereeing career and indeed my life, but first I want to take a step backwards more than 90 years to my childhood.

7   FATE TAKES A HAND

My deep love for football had begun in the fields surrounding the farmhouse of Cox Farm, off Little London Hill in Warnham, where I was born in December 1910. I was actually born in the barn there, for reasons I can't remember. This almost biblical beginning to my life is something that my family has constantly ribbed me about jokingly ever since.

It was a happy home for four years, where I had the run of the farm for a playground. My dad Ernest was from Barnet in North London but had been brought up as a farmer, a far cry from my mother's world of show business. Born Phylis Machin she came from Sunderland where her father was an impresario, owning a popular and highly successful music hall. The family moved to Spencers Farm in 1914, selling Cox Farm to the celebrated cricketer Percy Fender, who is best known for once hitting a century in an astonishing 35 minutes, still one of the fastest ever recorded.

As a talented all-rounder Fender, who died in 1985 at Exeter at 92, played 13 tests for England as well as a career spanning Surrey and Sussex. The great cricket writer E.W. Swanton, who would cross my path controversially in football circles, famously described Fender's bowling, with its unusual technique, as "beyond all laws" but he was also a useful right hand bat.

Dad had great ambitions for the family and wanted more land to farm, and he planned to build his herd and to expand the dairy business. I cherish warm memories of those distant days. The First World War was at its height then, though fortunately I was too young to have memories, as my parents did, of those grim days when the guns boomed across the Channel and men were slaughtered in the service of their country.

No, for me it was life on the farm where life was perfect and everything a small boy could have wished for. The enormous house had eight bedrooms and was so large that my family shared it with the Prewett family, who owned a flourmill in Horsham. The fields, the woods, and the streams were our environment. One side of our farmland was bordered by the Red River at Warnham and for a small boy it was a wonderful place in which to grow up.

At the age of ten I had my first paid job, as an apple boy. In the late summer and autumn it was my task to inspect and grade all the apples and pears that were picked from our two big orchards. They were gathered in large wicker baskets that were hauled up to the loft in the house. It was a weekly chore that took anywhere up to five hours to complete. But it was worth my time because it provided me with my pocket money and sometimes a bit of a bonus from Mr Carter, the greengrocer, who would call at 7.30 am on Monday mornings to collect all the fruit I had sorted. I will never be able to forget one of the evenings when I was working away in the loft.

Just as the light was fading and I was getting ready to go down the ladder there was the brightest flash of light and an enormous crash that seemed to shake the whole building. I thought it could only be an earthquake and with the two farm dogs close behind we came down from the loft without touching the stairs. I already knew how to swim and to skate, but that night I learned how to fly. As I came down my parents, ashen-faced, were on their way up and as we struggled to work out what was happening we heard the clanging of the bell on the town's fire-engine.

A neighbour had rushed to the fire station and led by their gallant captain – as well as being Horsham's most celebrated sportsman of the day and proprietor of Hunt Bros. department store, Mr Cyril Hunt, the crew were soon swarming over the house trying to find the cause of the tremendous explosion. Soon we had the answer, courtesy of Leading Fireman 'Duck' Etheridge, also captain of the Trinity football team.

It turned out to be in the rose bed, just a few feet from the front door of the house. Or rather the former rose bed, because now, in its place was a chasm, a gaping hole where, all agreed, a bolt of lightning must have struck. After a great deal of head-shaking the assembled company repaired to the kitchen where dad opened many bottles of beer and mother's supply of freshly-baked scones, which were intended to feed the farm for a week, seemed to disappear in a matter of moments.

The lively chatter around the big oak table soon turned to football and, in particular, the memorable match played only the day before between Trinity and arch rivals Crawley Comrades. Going into the final match of the season, the two teams were level on points at the top of the League, so the winners would get the spoils. A big crowd had been expected but few could have anticipated the hundreds who turned out to watch.

People came from miles around, all drawn by the prospect of a real derby match blood bath. The League knew what to expect too, because not only did they send the redoubtable F.C.Coates, our assistant Postmaster, to referee, but he even had two neutral linesmen, an unprecedented recognition of the importance of the match. Our family were all involved, me selling programmes and rosettes, and Mum making the green and white rosettes, which were sold for 5d each.

The huge crowd was drawn to the game not only because it would decide the Championship but also as it would see the debut of Trinity's secret weapon, the Reverend Mathews who had recently arrived in the Parish and who had won his Blue playing football for Oxford University. Within minutes of the kick-off the Comrades were a goal up but midway through the half the Reverend Mathews drove home a corker of a goal to the delight and relief of the home crowd.

With only moments to go before half-time Crawley scored again, so they had a 2-1 advantage when the teams changed ends. 'Duck' Etheridge made it 2-2 but before the crowd could draw breath to cheer Trinity on to victory the Comrades had scored again and the Championship seemed to be slipping away. Then, in the 70th minute, the Reverend Mathews set off on a mazy run towards their goal and, as he prepared to shoot, he was brought clattering down by the league's notorious 'hardman', Charlie Brooks.

The crowd went crazy as the referee cautioned Brooks. The Reverend, by now the darling of the crowd, placed the ball on the edge of the penalty area but his kick was mishit and instead of curling toward the onrushing Trinity forwards it flew straight at the referee, hit him on the shoulder and bobbled into the Crawley net. Yes indeed, God works in wondrous ways his miracles to perform. The Crawley Comrades went berserk throwing every player into attack but the Trinity defence held out for the remaining ten minutes and the match was won 4-3.

In front of an ecstatic crowd Mrs Nellie Victor Laughton presented 'Duck' Etheridge with the trophy and the huge crowd cheered and cheered. Our new vicar could not have made a better start to his new life in the parish, for his Sunday congregation proved to be bigger than any parishioner could remember for many a year. The re-telling of this celebrated match was enjoyed almost as much as the game itself, it seemed to me, and it was a happy crowd of firemen who, donning their shiny brass helmets, made their way back to their fire engine.

As Cyril Hunt and my dad headed toward the front door, Mr Hunt, sporting his silver fire chief's helmet, couldn't help but see the large shield leaning against the hallstand and dad proudly showed off the fruits of Trinity's labours of the previous afternoon, the Horsham League Trophy. Mr. Hunt, being a businessman down to his bootstraps, immediately spotted a marketing opportunity. He explained to Dad that on Monday the display windows in his department store were due for their monthly dressing and he would be happy to give pride of place to the trophy.

It would be a good attraction both for the store and for Trinity, the two men agreed. So, the following morning, along with the apples and pears, Mr Carter, greengrocer, found himself the proud conveyor of the Horsham League Trophy.

A few days later the peace of the evening was shattered once more by the furious clang of the fire engine's bell but this time it was not attending a fire, just delivering eighteen beautiful 'Peace' roses to mum, to plant out in her newly re-filled rose garden.

Such was life those eighty years ago. Little things meant a lot then. People cared for and about one another and for a small boy life was full of wonder. Soon I was to have a playmate as my brother, Basil, was born in 1915 and we would enjoy many happy years in one another's company including him being best man when I married for the first time. Sadly, Basil, who married and had children, died in his 40s, having survived being shot by a German plane during war service as a despatch rider in his 20s.

He only had the use of one lung after contracting a disease through inhaling a seed while we were playing in a hayfield as kids. One lung was completely black and they took it away. Then later they classed him A1 fit for the army, which was ludicrous. The daft thing was that I was much fitter than Basil but failed the medical when my time had come, and it saved my life.

A working farm is far from an ideal playground with its inherent dangers, as the fourth finger of my left hand still shows. Playing with other boys in one of the barns my finger proved no match for the flashing blade of a scythe and I was rushed to Horsham Cottage Hospital with the top joint almost completely severed. There was no alternative but to cut it off completely and I was soon the proud owner of a bandaged hand that made me the envy of all my chums.

Only four days later the Tarratt family was in the wars again, only this time it was my mother who needed help and it was much more serious. She came into the big, warm farm kitchen one morning with her arms full of bluebells that she had just picked from the woodland close to the house, intending to freshen the many vases of flowers that decorated the house. Much later, around about midnight, she was terribly feverish, short of breath and clearly suffering, so my dad went around to fetch the family doctor, Dr. Vernon, and bring him back to see mother.

We children sat below in the kitchen and waited as the adults rushed around upstairs and finally Dad re-appeared, helping the doctor to carry my mother to the motorcar. They drove through the night to St. Bartholomew's Hospital in London, Dr. Vernon having decided that mum needed emergency treatment that would not be available in Horsham. It seemed that she had a little cut in her arm, perhaps from working in the kitchen, and that sap from the bluebells had poisoned her blood.

Without Dr. Vernon's insistence on taking such dramatic action she would undoubtedly have died, and quite quickly too. Thankfully the crisis was soon over. After a long period of recuperation mother returned in good health, and life on the farm returned to normal. Sadly, my mother was fated to die relatively young, passing away at only 54, and her death left a huge hole at the centre of the family. Thankfully my father Ernest was granted the good fortune of a long life and was 95 when he died at his home in Goring in 1976, having found happiness again when he married his second wife Doris.

In his lifetime my father built many of the houses in the Horsham area, provided the pitch for Horsham Trinity Football Club at Redford Avenue, played at Horsham Bowling Club, belonged to the National Farmers Union, and was a churchwarden at Holy Trinity Church in Horsham. Those early years were indeed happy days and both my parents shared the task of ensuring that we enjoyed life as fully as we could.

I clearly recall how my friends and I would wait for news of the latest episode in the fabulous life of my Uncle William and how envious they all were of my having a real live cowboy in my family. He was my mother's brother, a rowing Blue at Oxford in 1914, who had emigrated to the USA and made his way to

Hollywood. He had fallen on his feet straightaway, landing a small part in a black-and-white silent picture.

From there Uncle William never looked back. He had always been a fine horseman and soon he was winning lead roles in a string of films. Billy Machin was our hero and we boys never tired of hearing about this living legend. But, sadly, he died when he was only in his mid 40's, his death caused, some said, by the damage he had done to his heart when training to row for his college and for Oxford University.

All this fed my dreams of heading off into the bigger world but for me it had to be football all the way. I had been bitten by the bug as soon as I had taken my first kick of a leather football at Collyer's School, Horsham, where I was enrolled when I was seven years old. I was hooked on the game from that first moment and quite determined that the school team would become the springboard for my footballing ambitions to become reality.

Collyer's School is now a well-known and highly-regarded sixth-form college, but in 1917 it was a public school taking boys from age seven until sixteen. I settled in to school life there quite happily but I had little interest in anything other than natural history and football, and I had a particular loathing for languages. Like every schoolboy there were teachers I looked up to and others who I could not abide.

Certainly my favourite was 'Pill' Robinson, deputy headmaster and a remarkable man. He would referee school football matches and he commanded the respect of all of the boys, which was surprising when I remember that he was no taller than 4 foot 3 inches tall and ran around the pitch in his striped school blazer, long black shorts wearing a black skull cap upon his head. 'Pill' also ran the school museum that was downstairs in what became the Cottage Hospital. He would call me from my lessons to help him with the nature exhibits because I am sure he recognised that I was never going to be a scholar but thought there was hope for me as a farmer.

On the farm we had a big pond close to the house and in there were enormous silver-grey newts. My dad helped me to construct a little holding tank within the pond and there I spent many happy hours studying those beautiful little creatures. Sadly, I don't suppose the children of today have such an opportunity and I doubt that their teachers have the time to spend in encouraging them to develop their interests in the way 'Pill' Robinson supported me.

One of my proudest moments came when I was officially appointed 'museum curator'. Perhaps I wasn't the finest scholar but I enjoyed my schooldays and I'm sure I benefited from those days in many more ways than show up in school exam results. 'Pill' would call on me to assist him in marking out the football pitches too – perhaps he knew even more about my future than even I give him credit for.

As I look back and remember the farm so warmly it is clear that it was not giving Dad all that he wanted from life. He finally decided he had enough of the land when he found himself up in front of the magistrate because one of the milkmen he employed had been selling something other than milk. What a scandal that prosecution was.

In those days the milk was delivered from the back of a horse-drawn cart and ladled into tin milk cans brought out into the street by the housewives along the route. It seemed that one of the roundsmen would regularly stop his cart by the bridge over the River Arun and allegedly he would top up the churn with river water.

Even though this was a long time before the days of food safety standards it was still recognised as a terrible risk to everyone's health, not to say something of a fraud. Thankfully for him dad was well connected in the town and the magistrates on the bench on the day of the hearing were luckily all his friends or acquaintances. The case was dismissed but obviously it was the final straw for dad and soon after he announced to the family that he was selling the herd and going into partnership with Tom Redford, a local builder.

Together they planned to use much of the farmland for new housing. In those days obtaining planning permission wasn't a problem – there was no such thing as 'green belt', and if there were any local concerns to deal with they were quickly addressed by Mr Redford who happened, rather conveniently, to be chairman of the local council.

As part of their agreement, a bungalow was built for the Tarratt family and at dad's insistence, a field was set aside for Trinity Football Club and plans were made to build a small pavilion there. Soon houses began to sprout all over Horsham. Springfield Park, Hillside, The Crescent, and scores of council houses should all have been worth a fortune to my Dad but somehow it did not work out that way and eventually the partners fell out.

There were arguments, then accountants and then lawyers and in the end where once the family had owned all the land that made up Cox Farm we found ourselves left with barely a penny. By now there were five mouths to feed. Dad, mum, me, Basil and most recently a third brother, Harry, who was born in December 1919. Harry eventually settled down to farming in Tasmania and died in 2003, followed a few days later by his wife. I was lucky enough to visit him three times and it's a beautiful place.

But before all this descended upon us we older boys, who once thought we'd take on the family farm, needed to pay our way in some other trade. So it was that in 1926, my schooldays over, that I realised that my future didn't lie in the way I thought it would and I needed to look around for a way to earn my keep.

I had no grand ambition; life was too full of football, tennis and all of the pleasures of life that are were on offer to an 18-year-old red-blooded male. I was one of the founders of Old Collerians AFC which took care of the winter whilst in the summer I played tennis at the Horsham Tennis Club and on the fine court of Mr Oddie the Town's Chief Magistrate, who lived in a lovely property in North Parade.

I had formed the Imps, a junior tennis club of the Horsham Conservative Association and he kindly let us play there. I went on to captain the Horsham Club for seven years, and I well remember competing in the Cranleigh Open playing doubles with Frank Newcombe, a tax inspector and a top class player. One year we put out the favourites who were from Surrey, but we did not get any further than that.

Then another time when I was playing alongside Ron Ragless in the Eastbourne Tournament we reached the quarter-finals. Ron was a fine footballer too, and at the time was playing centre forward for Horsham Football Club. My tennis greatly improved when I joined the elite Arun Club in the Bishopric. I had a good coaching from Captain Evans who was a top class player. Tony Smith was a member and so was Mary Hunt, who I partnered in several events.

Our most exciting times were matches were against the Horsham doctors, captained by Dr Dew Senior with Dr Bradford, Dr Morgan, and Dr Hitchins, when we usually finished neck and neck. Mary Hunt was the daughter of Cyril Hunt who owned Hunt Brothers, the beautiful department store in West Street, Horsham.

What a fine place that store was, with the liveried footman at the front door, and accommodation at the top of the building for the shop girls. That front door was a magnet for all the young men in Horsham on a Saturday evening. What wonderful days. Mr Hunt also captained the Horsham Fire Brigade and I too was a proud member of that gallant band. As soon as the brigade members heard the fire bell toll we were to drop whatever we were doing and make our way to the fire station as quickly as we could.

I remember wearily trailing home early one morning after a night fighting a hayrick fire. My mother took one look at the smoke-stained wretch in the kitchen doorway and threw me, still fully dressed, straight into the tinplate bath. She was most unimpressed with my excuses, only having eyes for the sorry state of the tennis whites I had been wearing since yesterday morning.

Thinking back it is hard to remember quite why I decided to become a dentist's assistant. Maybe it was the only job on offer but for eighteen months I spent my working day at Ellis Kent in the Carfax watching the people of Horsham nervously enter into the dentist's lair. Mr Kent was quite a character. He had lost one leg and the 'clump' of his wooden peg-leg across the floorboards struck fear into many of the patients who waited, quivering, for him to set about them with his evil-looking instruments.

One of those reluctant patients, I vividly recall, was my dad. He had no more love of dentists than anyone else, so by the time he came for treatment he was in a great deal of pain otherwise he would never have come near the place. Seventy years ago the dentistry profession was not too knowledgeable about hygiene and once a tooth was showing significant decay the only choice was extraction. So it was with dad that day, only in his case it was decided he needed to have all of his teeth removed in one session.

Well, if hygiene was not too developed neither was the science of pain killing. It was a three-man operation that day. Dad in the chair, the dentist hauling away as tooth after tooth reluctantly emerged from the blood-spattered mouth, and me sitting on the patient's chest, trying in vain to keep him still. Most of the Carfax must have known what was happening because in his agony, with arms and legs flailing, Dad managed to kick out the dentists "shop" window.

That certainly drew quite a crowd on the street outside, though I cannot believe it was much of an advertisement for the tender loving care of Ellis Kent, me included. Clearly dentistry was never going to be the career for me but what was I going to do? My social life had settled down and in 1936 at the age of 26, at St Mathias Church Brighton, I married Ivy "Billie" Blackman, an attractive Brighton girl who shared my enthusiasm for tennis and was a member of Horsham Tennis Club, of which I was captain.

The local paper reported that I was a member of the fire brigade, Round Table, and a special constable and that I was working as an agent for an insurance company. At the same time, Ivy, known always as Billie, had been living in Horsham for several years and working for ET Lane and Company in the town. Like it or not the time had come to put down some roots and so it seemed the perfect opportunity had come about when I got the offer to buy a grocery and sweet shop in Park Street, Horsham.

It was during our time running the shop that our daughter Sonia was born, soon after we married. The business was not doing well and clearly needed a bit of energy and effort if it was going to succeed. So Billie and I set about re-building trade. I used to deliver groceries every day. We had a very healthy route in Warnham, I remember, and we worked hard to bring new customers into the shop and to fight off the competition.

Of course these were days long before supermarkets. Our customers were almost all housewives and children. The mothers would pick out the fruit and vegetables the families needed for the next day or two, pay for them and later in the day the order would be delivered to their homes. These were times when people knew their neighbours, when children could play happily in the streets, and when strangers were greeted with a smile rather than a scowl and a slammed door.

Most of our customers left the back door of their home open so that could we leave the order on the kitchen table, trusting us just as much as we knew we could trust them. I happily remember the many children who used to drag their parents down to the shop on a Sunday morning. The craze of those times was the picture card packed in alongside the sweet cigarettes that were bought by children, the sweet versions looking much like the real cigarettes bought by adults.

On a Sunday we would be overrun by children swapping cards between each other and begging their parents for more pennies to buy more sweet cigarettes. Thinking back, I can picture the faces of the long-suffering parents as they reluctantly pulled a few more pennies from their pockets. One little face was particularly memorable, Peter Wilkins, whose name would crop up in my life on several occasions as the years passed by especially with regard to football, and with whom I have still had contact at the time of putting this book together.

Daughter Sonia had everyone worried when she got her finger stuck in a cigarette-dispensing machine, which left her screaming with pain. When she was examined it was found the poor little soul had lost the top of one finger and Sonia remembers that painful incident to this day. I was young and ambitious in those days and I happily rang up each sale on the gleaming cash till. The early 1930's were tough times in a little market town like Horsham though, and we took every opportunity we could find to earn extra money.

For a time I took on an insurance round which took me out in the evenings to sell new policies and collect payments from householders around Horsham. I have never been one to turn down an opportunity if it felt right, indeed if I had stuck quietly to the path of certainty and security I know I would never have experienced the many remarkable twists and turns that my life has taken.

So it was with football. Although I was a regular player for Trinity, I finally decided that I had to give up playing at 22 when it became clear that a knee injury I had picked up in my schooldays now threatened to cripple me for life. I had no difficulty in running but when I kicked a ball the pain in my knee was hard to bear. I had a few games playing goalkeeper but I knew I was only kidding myself and that each game I played was causing my knee to swell and to hurt quite horribly.

Dad paid for me to see a specialist, who was in no doubt that I should only expect matters to get worse if I carried on playing. What choice did I have? However important football was to me I knew that it would be plainly stupid to ignore his advice. Maybe I could referee though? It would keep me in touch with the game I loved so much.

I knew it would not be easy, particularly when I found myself back in the company of my old pals, as I surely would some day, but it would keep me in the game. So, like every other would-be 'man in black' of those times I was registered as a Class 3 referee, in my case for Horsham and District in 1932 and I was back on the pitch.

While I was obviously concerned with making a living and raising my family, my time as a referee began to play a big part in my life in the next 20 years or so. But first I had to cut my teeth, so to speak, in local football, and that could often spring a few surprises. Those 30s matches in local football left me with some strange memories that stayed with me as I moved up the ladder, my first step being appointed a Sussex County league referee in 1935.

My first county league match in the 35-36 season was a big moment for me although on the pitch it was uneventful. Unless, that is, you happened to be the goalkeeper for the Eastbourne Old Comrades, who let in five goals without his feeble forwards mustering a single reply against home side Worthing on 28 September 1935. Worthing were of course later destined to move up to a higher grade of football.

Within a year I found myself rather unwittingly making a small slice of local football history in a truly remarkable match at Bexhill's Polegrove ground on 31 October 1936, the like of which has probably never been equalled in County League circles to this day. I had to abandon a weird Sussex County league match there when visitors Littlehampton had only three (yes this is not a typing mistake, only three) players left on the pitch.

Without doubt it was one of the strangest matches I ever handled at any level. Such a bizarre scenario deserves a fuller explanation, and that was what I had to give the league later. They had never encountered such a problem before and I doubt they ever have since. What happened was the match was played in a gale and in such poor light that I had to order a quick turnaround at half-time in the vain hope of finishing in daylight, there being no floodlights.

Bexhill themselves had their own problems and had started with only ten players. Littlehampton fielded several reserves and were no match for even the depleted home side. When I blew for half-time the Littlehampton team dashed off the pitch into the gloom and, as I was to discover, had entirely lost their appetite for this lop-sided fixture. The time came a few minutes later to restart the match, but only six "Marigolds" as Littlehampton came to be known, were on the pitch as we prepared to kick off.

With light fading fast, I decided to re-start the game in the hope of getting it completed and thought the other players would return to the pitch soon. Instead we had the farcical situation of Littlehampton players leaving the pitch one by one without approval, despite my pleas for them to remain. Whether they were demoralised at being 4-0 down or just freezing cold, or both, I do not know to this day.

When it got down to three players on the visiting side the position was ridiculous so I abandoned the match with 25 minutes still to play, telling what was left of the Littlehampton team the result would stand. I forget after all this time what happened to the players who left the field but the three who had the decency to stay on were Speller in goal, Bennett the centre-forward, and Best the right-half, so I suppose you could say they had the spine of a team but nothing else. When a local reporter asked me what I thought of the whole bizarre episode I simply told him: "It was ridiculous to continue".

For the record, the Littlehampton team that wrote a piece of Sussex football history that day was Speller, White, Mobsby, Best, Beeching, Mann, Becket, Baker, Bennett, Cunningham, and Gibbons. Bexhill were: Hall, Billingham, Perry, George, Saunderson, Martin, Crane, Johns, Cheeseman, Lillycrop and Stevenson. Even Perry, the Bexhill left back grabbed a goal in this remarkable game. I suppose you could say it was a farce, but the County League is better run nowadays and I cannot think that such a thing would be allowed to happen.

In the 1930s in the lead-up to those terrible war years big crowds were drawn to local games. The tension and fiercely partisan nature of the crowds were great experience for the day when I would, eventually, officiate before more than 160,000 people at one single game. In those days people took supporting their local team very seriously. For many it was a big thing in the week, which might sound strange now, but it was true then.

Following the fortunes of County League clubs over the years in the media I wonder what size crowds clubs like Burgess Hill Town might have pulled if they had enjoyed their wonderful run of Sussex County League championship wins in the 1930s instead of achieving it in the last few years. Towns like Burgess Hill and Horsham are much bigger now, but interest in local football is not nearly as great.

I think I must be right about that, when people who are in touch with the county scene tell me that despite winning the County League five times in seven seasons up to 2003, which I think is a magnificent achievement, Burgess Hill drew an average crowd of about 200 to their Leylands Park ground.

And I hear they are one of the best-supported local teams. I gather Burgess Hill have left the County league in the current 2003-4 season for the higher grade of the Dr Martens Southern League, following the example of my local team Horsham in aiming for a better standard of football. I wish them luck, because everyone needs a fresh challenge and I hope their ambition is rewarded.

My interest in refereeing, both local and professional matches, led me to keep profiles and quotes of some referees, as a rather nostalgic look at my scrapbook about 40 years later reveals. Mind you, if I had taken to heart some lines by Jack Ingham, which I kept in my cuttings book, I think I would have been frightened to ever blow my whistle. One little nugget of advice from jolly Jack said: "No person anywhere, even a murderer, is hooted and jeered half as much." A referee must be able to keep calm while a huge crowd raves at him."

Undeterred I enjoyed taking charge of matches, and it helped me forget that what I would really have loved to be doing at such a young age was enjoying the comradeship of playing in a football team. In comparison, although I made many friends through refereeing, being in the middle is solitary. That might sound strange, but even in front of a huge crowd of 40,000 or more you can feel very alone. It is not necessarily a negative thing,

I always enjoyed the responsibility even if things went a bit pear-shaped, but at best you are part of very small team of three, with your two linesmen. Still thriving with the whistle, by the time I was 27 I had been appointed linesman for Football League and FA Cup matches, at the time being the youngest ever on the list. Brighton and Hove Albion, who have featured a lot in my football life, nominated me for the promotion, as was the procedure in those days.

It was with some pride that I then looked at First Division programmes and saw my name printed there as one of the linesmen, on the same pages as famous players worshipped by the fans. One of the greatest names I came across was Matt Busby, then with Liverpool, who played right half against Chelsea on Christmas Eve 1938 when I ran the line. Every football fan knows he built three great Manchester United teams, but he was a superb player as well and his class as a footballer and a person stood him in good stead throughout his eventful life.

Matt Busby's wonderful record as a manager has to some extent been eclipsed by Alex Ferguson's remarkable run of championship wins for United in the 1990s and early 2000s. People forget that but for losing most of his team in the Munich air crash Busby would almost certainly have been able to sit back in his office and watch his incredible still-maturing young side win the European Cup, the League and the FA Cup many times during the next ten years. It is one of sport's great enduring tragedies that we shall never know.

In other games I came across Frank Swift the wonderful Manchester City and England goalie with the huge and safe hands. He was one of the best ever and a marvellous man as well, and I was sad to read later in life that he died in the Munich air crash while working as a journalist. Watching "Big Swifty" plunging around in goal I could never have imagined such a cruel ending for him.

Cliff Bastin, who was in the Arsenal side that became the first southern team to win the League in season 1930-31, was still doing the business on the left wing for them in September 1939 when I lined up for a 5pm kick-off at Highbury against Sunderland. Bustling Ted Drake, who was utterly fearless on a football field, was centre-forward for Arsenal and he was unlucky that there were so many good centre-forwards around, otherwise I think he would have played a lot more games for England.

Drake scored six goals in five England matches and of course wrote himself into the record books when he scored all seven of Arsenal's goals in their 7-1 win at Aston Villa despite having his damaged knee strapped up. The knee later needed an operation. In the Arsenal side that day against Sunderland was the 25-year-old Bryn Jones, who had been signed to do almost the impossible and replace the incomparable Alex James.

It didn't help poor Jones that "moneybags" Arsenal, as they were called then, had forked out a record £14,000 for him. This created a huge fuss in the media and although at his best he was a fine player with a lovely passing range I think

Jones lost too much of his career to the war years. In the Sunderland ranks that day was the revered captain and inside-right Raich Carter, who had helped Sunderland to their first FA Cup final in 1937, beating Preston 3-1.

Soon much more serious matters would be concerning everyone with the War, but for the time being we enjoyed what we could of the great football that was on show. I admired many of the players I refereed, but people have often wondered if some players took a disliking to me over the years. Well, I cannot pretend every player I came across liked me and they certainly did not always agree with my decisions. However, it was, as far as I can remember, purely a professional disagreement and most of the personal abuse was left to the crowds to dish out.

Yes, I like to think I got on well with some of the players. I will not say I had any special knack, but I used to be very friendly with so many players, like Sam Bartram, the Charlton goalkeeper. Sam used to ring me up and say would I like to go round London on a bus. Sam knew every statue and every road and we used to go up there and have lunch, and then we would go round on the ordinary buses. He was a walking timetable, always seemed to know which bus to catch where. A lovely man, he was, too.

There is a well-told story that old Charlton fans might recall that Sam once played with a poultice on his stomach to get him through an FA Cup semi-final with Newcastle after contracting food poisoning just before the game. I don't know what that treatment was supposed to do for him, but Charlton went on to win the Cup so maybe his doctor should have got a winners medal as well as Sam.

Jumping ahead a bit, I was delighted when Sam got some deserved praise when I turned up to do the West Bromwich and Charlton match in September 1953. Football has always been a hard, competitive business, but West Brom were kind enough to remind the crowd in their programme that loyal Sam had been 19 seasons with Charlton and they added: "His red head seems almost as much part of Charlton as their red shirts."

No one could have summed it up better and Sam was one of those blokes you count yourself lucky to have come across in your life. It was great moment for him and for me when he made his 500th appearance for Charlton in 1954 in a game against Portsmouth and set what was then a league record. One of my proudest possessions is the photograph of me you can see in this book refereeing in front of more than 60,000 people at the Valley, with Sam leaping through the air in the foreground.

If you haven't been out in the middle, either as a player or ref, in front of crowd like that it's impossible to get across what it actually feels like. Except that it is bloody marvellous.

As I pause sometimes to reflect on my life I think of the many great players I saw up close in my time.

Of them all, Alex James was easily the best footballer, because he had such an immense amount of skill and a natural lovely touch on the ball.

It would have been all too easy to stand and watch this man play football all day, it seemed the game had been invented for him. Modern football fans will probably have no idea what I am talking about and it is a shame for them that no videos and DVD recordings exist of Alex. He was the equal of anyone playing in Britain today, and I do mean anyone. Joe Mercer stays in my mind as being brilliant, surely one of the best ever, and I say that even though he was really nasty to me at times during that momentous 1951 Manchester United match. To be fair, on every occasion I came across him after that he was fine.

The peerless Johnny Carey of Manchester United, who I mentioned earlier, was getting on in the 1950s but he must have been one of the coolest, most versatile and greatest players ever for United. He struck me as being a gentlemanly sort of player, but he could dish out a hard and decisive tackle on the rare occasions his powers of interception let him down. My memory of him is reading a pass almost before it left an opponent's boot, moving into the space, taking the pace off the ball however hard it seemed to be hit, then playing it quickly and perfectly weighted to a winger's feet.

Carey hated belting the ball anywhere on the park, although he had enough dynamite in his boots to clear the stand if he needed to. In fact Carey was so good that one of the reporters at that game I did at Highbury in 1951, Maurice Smith, not only named him man of the match but wrote: "Manchester United's captain is the complete footballer-surely one of the truly great of all soccer history." Having seen him at close quarters, I wouldn't argue about that.

Elegant Roger Byrne, who I mentioned earlier, was one of the few full-backs to regularly shackle Stan Matthews, so that speaks for itself. Whenever I think of a defender trying to cope with Stan Matthews it brings to mind lines from that old song that goes Bewitched, Bothered, and Bewildered. They knew what he was going to do to them, and he did it anyway.

I came across him at Aston Villa when Blackpool were playing Tottenham in the semi-final of the Cup and Blackpool won. I think they won by two goals to one. I was senior linesman and Arthur Ellis, a very famous referee, was in the middle.

I have never seen a player like Matthews. He was the best winger I ever saw. He was so tricky and beautifully balanced. He was more like the foreign players today, the way he'd trap a ball and keep control of it, and his dedication to fitness. He seemed to absolutely have the ball glued to the end of his boot, even when he was running at speed. And he was a lovely man, a real gentleman and so devoted to playing.

He was not big-headed, there was no cockiness there, nothing like that, although of course he was confident about his own ability and good Heavens he used it. It did not matter if the defender knew what he was trying to do, because he was so good. He was selfish at times, he hung on, but after the tackle had gone in he still had the ball. And he went to the by-line before pulling the ball back, which was a big problem for defenders trying to cut the ball out.

It's probably true that nowadays they would get defenders to gang up on him, but like George Best, who I think was the nearest we got to a perfect all-round British footballer in modern times, he would have found a way. They used to say Stan disappeared from games, but he usually re-appeared to create havoc. Even if he had a bad game, which was unusual, the crowd loved to wait in expectation of one of his runs. The buzz used to hum around the terraces when Stan shaped for a dribble, and it was an unforgettable sight and sound.

As well as great footballers I sometimes came across great referees when I ran the line. In November 1950 I had the honour of lining for one of the best, Arthur Ellis, in Paris for the thrilling 3-3 draw between France and Belgium at the Stade de Colombes. I still have the letter from Stanley Rous asking me to cover the game, which was my first international appointment on the line. I treasure that letter to this day.

The same year in a vastly different setting a 10,000 crowd in Guernsey sang Sussex By The Sea to me as I walked out to referee the passionately fought inter-island championship match. That was a very moving moment for me. It was lovely, and very kind of them. The game was won 2-1 by Rangers of Guernsey against Old St Paul's. of Jersey. I had two local linesmen with me, and I was over there with Mr Fred Gates, who was the postmaster in Horsham and secretary of the Horsham League, and he really loved that weekend.

In those days my second wife Edith went to quite a few of the games, and sometimes took young Rodney along and I used to hope I did not get too much offensive abuse, though obviously I sometimes "copped it "from the crowd. Football fans can be a bit aggressive and stupid and hopelessly one-sided in what they see, but I think the best of them know a good deal more about the game that some people inside the professional game give them credit for. I know everyone is hell bent on winning now, but the real football fans have always as long as I can remember liked to see a good game for their money too. They do pay an awful lot for their football now.

Although I took a good deal of personal abuse over the years, I do admire the passion of fans for their teams, although I hate any form of crowd violence or foul language. I wish supporters would concentrate more of supporting their own side and less on taunting opposing fans, which is negative and can start trouble, but that's probably hoping for too much in the real modern world.

For that hard-fought game in the Channel Islands I was sporting new canvas and rubber referees boots which were far more comfortable than stiff leather and this attracted a considerable amount of publicity, although I cannot recall if sales of the boots soared after this free press "plug".

This game was brilliantly covered by the local papers, with pictures of every player, and it shows just how much football meant to people even at non-Football League levels in those days.

It is hard for people to realise nowadays just how much enthusiasm there was for the game then. What I admire is a real passion for the game and usually a sporting acceptance of defeat. I won't say things were always rosy then, players were poorly paid and there were still plenty of scoundrels on the pitch able to use those heavy boots they used to wear to clog the Matthews and Finneys of this world, that's if they caught them.

As I left after that Guernsey match the crowd was able to buy a full two-page report of the match they had seen only a few minutes earlier, so the local press moved pretty quickly in those days. Back in Sussex, I trained at least once week at the Albion's Goldstone Ground in Hove, and I found myself back there blowing a whistle on 9 May 1951 when the FA was staging a series of FA

Jubilee Festival of Britain games. Albion beat Nancy of France two goals to one and it was an honour to do the match for the club.

The French created a bit of a stir by including two Argentinians in their team and we didn't see many of them in the UK in those days. The same year on Monday 3 September I was able to repay George Cox's friendship and kindness to me by refereeing his benefit match between Horsham and Arsenal, which drew a crowd of 4,700, at the time the third highest in Horsham's history. The crowd had the thrill of seeing Alex James, one of the most revered and talented players ever to wear an Arsenal shirt, who I have talked about before, come out of retirement to honour his former Gunners team-mate and Sussex cricketer.

In fact, there were four county cricketers named for Arsenal's team that day. This was in the times when football did not swamp the calendar and there was a football season and a cricket season, and some famous names excelled at making a living at both. During my refereeing travels I came across the amazing Compton brothers, Les and Denis, who both played for Middlesex and for Arsenal with great distinction.

Both those Compton brothers played international football for England, but left-winger Denis, who scored nearly 40,000 first-class runs, was by far the more brilliant cricketer and made the England team. I think he would have played more if football injury hadn't stopped him. Les, a reliable centre-half, had the unusual distinction of making his England football debut at 38 in 1950. Neither could pursue such fascinating dual careers now because cricket is squeezed by a football season that takes up most of the year.

Jack Kelsey was in goal for Gunners and they had five other first team regulars in Barnes, Bowen, Roper, Lewis, and Shaw so a 4-2 defeat for Horsham was a respectable effort. Horsham's Pope and Parker had the honour of scoring against the mighty Arsenal, something a few first Division forwards could not achieve that season, although it has to be said that against Horsham silky Arsenal relied more on their far superior passing and ball control rather than over-exerting themselves physically.

The crowd "purred" at some flashes of quick passing and instant control from the Gunners which surpassed anything they saw on a Saturday from their local heroes, even though Horsham were a very tidy team in the county. They got good value, and I seemed to have won a friend with the local sports reporter who said in his write-up: "Ralph Tarratt is to be congratulated in refereeing in such a masterly and fearless style." Perhaps that was a little, as they say, "over the top" in praise for what was essentially a pleasant friendly match but it was nevertheless a kind thought and better for a man's morale than some of the insults, fruit, and "veg" that came my way over the seasons.

8   PERIL IN SOUTH AMERICA

With also refereeing amateur internationals in this period leading up to the mid-50s I was enjoying football, my marriage, and our business, and I was working hard at them all. That fateful Arsenal-Manchester United Division One game in 1951 that began my tale at the start of this book would now transform my refereeing life and take it to a new level.

In July 1953 I flew to Argentina for what turned out to be one of the greatest games of my life. As I remember, this appointment began as a result of Stanley Rous being impressed by my performance as stand-in referee in that Arsenal match two years before. Luckily for me, he never really forgot that, and I stayed on pretty close terms with him, and visited his home. One thing that I can still recall about him even after so long, and it has nothing to do with football, is that he was the most marvellous dancer. Like they seem to say about footballers on the television nowadays, he had great feet. He was certainly very nimble when it came to a samba.

There was always something of the patronising former schoolmaster about him in his manner, although he was great man and always pleasant to me. He never once in all the years I knew him called me Ralph. It was always: "Hello Tarratt." I flew with him to Buenos Aires as part of the team of match officials for the Argentina-Spain match. At that time British referees were regarded as the best in the world, and some were even offered jobs in Argentina.

The previous year I had officiated when Argentina were invited to play hosts Portugal to open their new national stadium and I remember the wonderful few days I spent with a couple of their top officials who owned vineyards, and one later came to Horsham to speak to the referees association. About that time there was sadness to me and immense grief to millions of people in Argentina over the death of Eva Peron, who had spoken with her usual passion at a function about the way money was being put it football in Argentina. As anyone who has seen photographs of her knows, she was very beautiful but of course as the cancer developed she looked terribly ill. I thought she was very brave.

At the time I did the Argentina game our referees were so highly regarded in South America that they were being fixed up with employment and provided with accommodation, and I suppose I might have been tempted. In fact, while I was out there I received an approach from the Mexican FA to live out there and handle some of their league games. I was with Sir Stanley Rous at the time and he took me to one side and advised me: "Don't do it. You have a good career in front of you." and I never regretted taking his advice and politely turning down the generous offer.

Sir Stanley could be a bit clever with you, though. He was a bit crafty. When we were on that plane to Buenos Aires for the Argentina game he came down the aisle and leaned over us and said: "I'm going to tell you now that last time these two teams played the game was never finished. It was an absolute shambles, there was fighting everywhere."

It was not exactly what we wanted to hear, but we still looked forward to the game. You see, the match they had played seven years before had just been the hell of a bloodbath. Now there was this huge crowd of 160,000 waiting for me and maybe one or two old scores were going to be settled. When I came out on to the pitch it was very exciting, but my job was to keep cool and calm, although there was the most tremendous wave of noise. To add to the pressure for the home players, sport and politics were bound tightly together in Argentina, so the Government's popularity rode on the back on sporting success. especially on the football pitch.

You do not go over the top emotionally in those situations, or you would lose concentration. That happened to a lot of players when I was refereeing. They blew their top either at me, an opponent, or even a team-mate, lost their grip on the game and made silly mistakes. Players need passion, but the best keep themselves under control.

The thing that sticks in my mind now from that Buenos Aires match was the seething mass of a crowd surging on to the pitch when a goal by Argentina was disallowed. I had been involved in some big games with crowds of nearly 70,000 in England but I'd never been in the middle of anything like this before. I thought this vast bowl of a stadium was going to empty on to the pitch and swamp us all. I started to look for a way out of it all as the tide began to surge from the steep terraces.

There was a moat around the pitch that was supposed to keep them off, but they smashed up seats and used them as some sort of makeshift bridge across the moat. Up until then I was not worried, not a bit. But I think I was when that crowd came on the pitch. The army and police were supposed to stop them coming on but they helped them over. I should think there were 300 army and police officers to control the crowd.

But they were the buggers that helped them over the moat, which as I stood on the pitch I do not think was very helpful in this situation I found myself. The game was held up for about 12 minutes. It was so blatant an invasion of the pitch and total chaos for a while. The West Sussex County Times had billed this trip on the front page of the 26 June 1953 issue before my departure from Horsham with the headline "Be a ref and see the world."

Somehow at that precise moment just past High Noon in Buenos Aires I felt I was seeing a bit too much of it for my own good. Boot Hill seemed to beckon. Argentina had thought they had scored and that is purely and simply what caused it. They must win at all costs over there. But thank heavens for Ernesto Grillo, who scored for Argentina just before half-time and gave them a 1-0 win. He should still be on my Christmas card list.

After that goal, we were made for life with the home fans. In fact, apart from the crowd invasion it was not an especially difficult game. The players themselves were not too much trouble. I was always looking out for the usual tricks over there in South America, diving and elbowing. I was not frightened or nervous. You felt fired up like the players. The football was brilliant, they were more skilful than the English League players and used much shorter passing. The long passing game wasn't their game. But they were crafty, and stretched the laws to the limit.

They certainly used their elbows a lot and rather dangerously. They also tripped with great cynicism the clever forwards who tricked them using superior skill, a foul that unfortunately we see regularly in modern football over here now. They were first to perfect it. Out there in the heat they and their tempers fuelled the rougher stuff.

That Argentina-Spain match was the biggest one of my life in terms of the size of the crowd and it was an honour for me to be officiating in South America. Perhaps Sir Stanley had given me that warning on the plane to keep us all on our toes. If he was, I suppose it worked, but we did not need much firing up once we walked out in front of that crowd.

Before we went to South America Sir Stanley had invited us to his home for dinner to discuss the trip. Of course, it sounded a marvellous opportunity and that is what it turned out to be. But he kept his dark secret until he got on the plane. It is a funny thing about huge crowds, like we had for the Argentina game, that you do not notice them during the match. You are concentrating too much.

After the match I had the tremendous honour with fellow official Arthur Luty of meeting President Peron, who of course lived long after the death of his wife, the famous Evita. Peron's politics were very much tied up with being promoting the excellence of the nation through success at sport and I guessed that the players must have been under a lot of pressure. We had quite a conversation although after so long it's difficult to remember everything that was said.

Peron was supposed to be a football fan of sorts, although it wasn't his favourite sport. I remember he spoke some English and I do remember afterwards he said something like: "You have done a good job, we are delighted with the result" which he obviously was because his team had won. Then he asked how long were we staying and we said we wanted to get back in two weeks.

Football was number one there, it seemed even above religion. They just worshipped the players, although they are a very religious nation. From what the Perons had been saying about developments there it appeared that the Argentinian government wanted to keep people happy and one way was to plough as much money as possible into football.

The fees for the South America trip were pretty good. When we went to the local football headquarters we were sitting there and the treasurer came up and told us we would get the equivalent of £250. I looked across at Sir Stanley Rous and he said: "Yes, take it. It's usual." And we took it, and bought presents for our wives. It was lot of money in those days but they didn't worry about money.

Officiating before this many people was one of the great moments of my life. The trouble for me was that there were English referees out there and they got so nasty with us because we had been sent over there and Spain would not let them in that game because they had been refereeing all over Argentina. They were old referees, English league referees. But they were a pretty fit lot, generally. Our English referees out there didn't like it, because we had pinched the Argentina-Spain game from them.

There were about seven out there and they were earning a lot of money from the game. Money was no object. Two were schoolmasters teaching English and the others worked for the Government, they got well paid and of course they got very good fees for refereeing. Their own referees in Argentina, you see, were eaten up with bribery. That was the trouble. That is why they set this up.

It was a lovely hotel we stayed at for that Argentina game, the best one in the city. But the one we stayed in for the next match, in Chile, was very stark, and entirely different. It was supposed to be a classy one, but everything was so ordinary. One thing I remember about Sir Stanley was that the girls used to swarm around him. He was a brilliant dancer, as I said, wonderful. He showed that in the night-clubs, night after night.

Even before I got back to Horsham from South America news of that crowd invasion had reached England through news agency reports. The West Sussex County Times of 10 July 1953 reported in a rather understated manner that I had "a rather exciting time in Buenos Aires on Sunday, according to agency reports.

"Linesman in the international between Argentina and Spain he was consulted by referee Arthur Luty when the latter disallowed an Argentinian goal in the second for offside. Mr Tarratt agreed with the referee- and then the fun started.
"The crowd, which had rushed on to the pitch to cheer the goal-scorer, diverted their now-angry attentions to the referee. More than 200 police had to push the protesting crowd from the pitch."

Before arriving for the match I was involved with, Spain had had some tough luck in getting knocked out of the preliminaries for the 1954 World Cup, losing in a two-team group to Turkey after a play-off and the toss of coin. World Cups were rather more "shambolic" then in their organisation and nothing like the massive competition it is now.

Argentina, who of course had a fine side in the early 50s, had not entered in 1950 after a bit of a "dingdong" with Brazil and when I arrived in 1953 had not entered for the 1954 World Cup either, so it looked like both they and Spain were at a loose end.

I followed Spain to Santiago a week later where they played Chile, and I very much enjoyed refereeing that game. Spain were desperate for a win so they wouldn't fly home to their fans empty handed and soon set about Chile with their pace and skill. There were some lovely touches in that game, some pure class that it was a privilege to snatch glimpses of as I refereed.

As a match, it was a lot more peaceful than the Argentina game but getting there over the Andes was a bit scary. The game was played at the national stadium with about 75,000 in the crowd.

Spain beat Chile 2-1, the same score Chile had lost to England a few months before. I kept the Chile-Spain programme dated 12 July 1953 to this day; it grieves me that I lost the Argentinian one. Anyway, it was a relief and gratifying for me that a press report referred to the "excellent manner in which Mr R.Tarratt of Sussex controlled the game."

To my consternation, we had to fly over the beautiful but menacing Andes in a pretty rough old plane to that Chile match, but once we got there the view of the mountains was fantastic. The bit that made me a little nervous was that we had to have two attempts at getting over the Andes because the weather was so bad and it was very windy. They had had several air crashes in the area so they were going carefully. It was an old propeller plane and I remember we had to pull down oxygen lines from the ceiling.

I was not terrified, but I wasn't especially relaxed either a few miles up in that old crate and I was certainly glad to land in Chile. In those days the pilots had to fly planes manually, they really had to handle them, without all the computer guidance you get now. It was a lovely football ground in Chile, but I was told it was where recent atrocities connected with the Government had been committed. The spectators there on this much happier day in 1953 arrived with their picnic baskets and they had acrobats and shows to entertain them. It went on from about 11 o' clock until kick off time at 3pm. and I remember they also had a boys game to entertain the crowd.

Playing for Chile in the game that I handled was George Robledo then 27, listed in the programme as Jorge, who had spent some time in England and spoke good English. He said to me, looking across at the players, "If you have any trouble come to me and I will speak to them." However, thankfully I didn't need him.

I remembered George, who had scored the winning goal FA Cup final goal for Newcastle the year before and made Newcastle the first side that century to retain the cup. In that game Joe Mercer, who was not in the prime of his youth, had fought valiantly to stop a ten-man Arsenal losing.

It was strange to see George out there on the pitch in the searing heat of Santiago after his star turns in the First Division, where he got 91 goals for Newcastle. In fact, he scored more goals per game than their big hero Jackie Milburn, though he did not play for Newcastle as long.

His brother Ted was out there with him, they had both left England in 1953 to play for the Chilean champions Colo Colo in Santiago so they didn't have far to go for the international. Not bad for two ex-Barnsley players I thought. Actually Ted, whose real name was Eduardo, was thought the lesser player and when Newcastle paid out about £26,000 for the pair and the talk was that they were more interested in George, although Ted did get into the team at half-back.

I think George averaged about one goal every two games, which was pretty good going. It was good to see his friendly smiling face out there in distant Santiago that day in the searing heat, and afterwards I thought of the winter days he must have slogged through the mud in Britain. The game in Santiago was a match I was not too happy about regarding my standards as a referee. I am sure I failed to give an offside that I should have spotted and given.

I gave a goal but afterwards I was suspicious about the decision. However, that was the only goal that Chile scored so it did not matter a lot. I think every referee must go through the game in his or her mind afterwards. I used to run it through perhaps when I was in bed, sometimes thinking I might have made a mistake. You should learn from looking at your mistakes, not just in refereeing of course but in life generally, though at my age I can't help thinking it's better to learn from someone else's if you can.

I certainly knew I was not positioned right on that occasion. It was an easy game for me. But I think it was in another game there poor old Ken Aston, who became chairman of the FIFA referees committee, got "murdered" when all hell broke loose in the 1962 World Cup match between hosts Chile and Italy and he sent two players off in one of the most violent World Cup matches on record. I think it was after his experience of that game, which was called the battle of Santiago, and the sending off of Argentina captain Rattin in the 1966 World Cup against England that he got the idea of bringing in red cards to improve communications where there were language barriers.

He said once that he saw the traffic lights changing colour and that gave him the idea of the different colour cards of red and yellow, which were later adopted. Like most brilliant ideas, it was simple and it worked.

Our third game in South America was the most volatile and it was not even an international. We took a short trip over the border to Fray Bentos, which sits right on the border of two countries, a city pretty close to the Argentinian border. Although it is in Uruguay, the team in Fray Bentos, presumably because they were so close to the border, played in the Argentinian league at the time. For a long time, possibly because of geography and economics, and even until about ten years ago, the top league in Uruguay was centred almost solely on the capital Montevideo.

It was mighty River Plate who were visiting Fray Bentos that infamous day in my career. They had won the title eight times before including the previous year and from what I saw of them they were ready to do anything to hang on to it, although I have to admit they had plenty of skill as well as being tough. They actually won the league eventually but not before some pretty nasty stuff on the pitch that day.

If it was excitement I was looking for I got plenty. The crowd was no-where near as big as the other games, perhaps about 40,000 but it was a real frightener. I remember River Plate won although I cannot recall the score but I had to send four men off and I was pleased to get away from the ground in one piece.

One other thing that stays with me about that trip to Fray Bentos, and it had nothing to do with football, was that as soon as the train got near to Fray Bentos there was a terrific smell of dead animals. I have never forgotten it. The game itself was certainly a bit of a carve-up. But luckily I had two good linesmen to help me, which is crucial to any game.

There was such a lot of dirty play in that game including pulling shirts. It was everything in the book really. It was the nastiest match I ever refereed. They were at each other the whole game and I was soon right in the middle of the roughest match of my life. It's a long time ago now and I can't remember why I sent the players off, but I remember elbows and legs seemed to flying around nowhere near the ball.

I feared someone would be seriously hurt, but just as alarming to me was that most of the players seemed to accept what I thought were some pretty frightening fouls. Believe me, I had seen some tough football in the Football League, especially in the lower divisions, where a few defenders were not slow to put the boot in. But these British players seemed like "pussycats" compared with what I was seeing in South America.

They were at each other's throats as they came out. You could see we were in trouble. The linesmen would sort of come in and protect you in a game like that. I got well and truly hammered by the crowd. I got the feeling they were after our blood. The police would not let us out after the game because they feared for our safety. It was three hours before they led us to a car. Fortunately, our car had been parked under the stand so it was all right because we could reach it fairly easily.

Although Fray Bentos is known almost solely for the corned beef brand it got its name from a hermit who followed religion about 300 years ago. I would have given anything to have been a hermit when the crowd was at its most hateful in that game. The city seemed to have to have a more positive English connection than yours truly Ralph Tarratt because we had something to do creating the meat processing industry in the early 1900s, and the locals liked to joke they fed half the USA army in World War Two.

The meatpacking factory had its own little community including a hospital and school. I was told about 500 cows an hour and about 1500 sheep a day were processed, as the locals put it. The old joke over there, often repeated since, was that the only thing they did not use from a cow was the moo. When I arrived and smelled the processing plant it had me been longing for the sunny white beaches I had heard about. In the end I was just glad to leave it all behind, but I never regretted the experience of that ferocious game.

There was an amusing follow-up to that South America trip which makes me smile even today.

After the Argentina game Sir Stanley said he was not coming back with us, he was going up country somewhere. We were told a steward would meet us when we got off the plane at Heathrow. Sir Stanley said a driver would take me back to Horsham but there were certain things he wanted me to take back with me. We spent the rest of trip home wondering what on earth he meant.

We arrived as arranged and this man was waiting for us after the bags had come off the plane. He said there was quite a lot of stuff for us to take. In fact there were 17 ladies handbags all made of crocodile skin. It appeared that a man in Peru had a crocodile farm. These bags were worth a fortune; they were absolutely the tops. He gave my son Rod's wife one, I do not know where the rest went, but he did have a lot of women admirers.

When Sir Stanley got back to England he said "Will you meet me on Saturday, bring your wife and Rodney to tea at the Grand Hotel in Brighton and of course bring the luggage with you."

The bags were superb, in white boxes, real Harrod's material.

9 GREAT NAMES AND SPORTING REFLECTIONS

South America was a wonderful experience for me and all through my career I loved the bigger crowds.

The crucial thing about being a referee, as far as I was concerned, was that we were trained to treat Horsham League games in front of a few people with as much concentration as the big Division One matches before thirty thousand or more. Long before the South America trip, a newspaper carried a story about me being the only Football League referee in Sussex and a reporter asked me if I was worried about crowds baiting officials. I told him, and I have the cuttings to remind me: "The bigger the crowd the better.

"It is when there are only a few spectators that the naughty remarks are heard by the referee and linesmen. In any case spectators have a right to their opinion, and their attendance at matches keeps the game alive".

A few referees who had great technical knowledge and were marvellous blokes never got used to working in front of big Football League crowds and lost their confidence, which was a great shame because it often stopped their progress. I suppose in some ways it is a bit like a footballer who can do his stuff at a lower level or dazzle in training but freezes at top grade.

I will never forget one afternoon when I was at Fulham and we were ready to go out and one of my linesmen looked at the other linesman, took me to one side and whispered: "That chap is trembling, he cannot even do his laces up." When I looked, it was true. He was absolutely bloody useless, and I had to report him to the League. He never made a League referee, which saddened me but standards had to be as high as possible.

Back home from my South American travels after summer 1953 I was again mixing League and local football and of course putting a lot of hours into the bar billiard table business, which involved a fair amount of socialising, and I was being kept pretty busy. The local press was pushing for me to be given an English FA Cup final, but with so many fine referees around I never achieved that, to my great disappointment.

When I got back from South America the Horsham-based West Sussex County Times, which has always shown an interest in my career, said: "Ralph Tarratt's latest honour strengthens the hopes of those of us who would like to see him in charge of a Wembley game. It is clear the FA high-ups regard his ability highly." All I can say fifty-odd years later to the newspaper is: "Thanks for trying."

Taking in the county games as well as top professional football I was able to see over the years small clubs gradually climb the ladder, like Crawley, and some champions, like Haywards Heath, gradually fall from the top flight.

The great thing about football is that teams can come good again as the promotion of the once mighty then fallen Portsmouth and Wolves into the 2003-4 Premier league shows. Having seen them at close quarters in their pomp it is nice to see them both climb back to the top level. Pompey even topped the Premier League briefly in August 2003, although with Chelsea spending more than £100 million on new players and Arsenal and Manchester United scrapping it out yet again Pompey have no chance of the title and I should think they would be very happy with mid-table.

It might surprise 21st century followers of Crawley Town, who now play senior non-league football at the impressive Broadfield stadium, to know that they were rock bottom of the Sussex County League Division One when I refereed their evening game against Bognor in April 1955, while Bognor were going strongly for the title. Both clubs have made great progress since then and it shows what can be achieved with a little ambition and drive, and in the case of Crawley a sports-minded council.

Crawley have a fine pitch now, but older supporters and surviving players will no doubt recall that Town Mead was a dismal mud-heap in the winter and must have drained the legs of players. Facilities for supporters were not much better but they are excellent now.

You have read in previous chapters some of the highlights of my refereeing career and it was a wrench when I had retire from top class officiating in 1955-56 season because I had reached the then upper age limit of 45. Yet the lure of the whistle stayed with me and I continued to enjoy refereeing in local league and charity matches and helping run the local association for a few more years, when the bar billiards table business really started to demand a lot more of my time.

My remarks earlier about hearing shouts from smaller crowds came to haunt me when, after leaving Football league matches behind me, I did a Corthinian League match at Woodside Road, Worthing, between Worthing and Dorking.

The depressing and somewhat amazing scenario for home supporters as we went into the last minute of this match was that it was already January and Worthing had not yet won a single League game. So there was unconfined joy when the Worthing centre forward headed in a centre in the dying seconds from about a yard. The Worthing players quickly ran back to re-start the game (there was not so much cuddling and daft showing off to the crowd in those days) and the supporters cheered wildly.

It took a few seconds for them to realise that I had ruled out the goal for a push on a Dorking defender, but they soon woke up in their fury. Woodside Road was a far more intimate ground than Buenos Aires and when the Evening Argus of 21 January 1957 reported I was booed off the field after that game it was being rather restrained. My ears stung from the various forms of verbal abuse as I left the field, although to the crowd's credit there was no physical threat. I had left the really big crowds and the top games behind but I was still enjoying being the man in black.

But by the time the swinging Sixties arrived, it was not only the end of my refereeing days but brought a huge change in society as Beatlemania and much more liberal attitudes to life began to grip Britain. Football would never be the same again either, especially after England won the World Cup in 1966 with what were called wingless wonders.

The traditional formation of two full-backs, three half-backs, two wingers, a centre-forward, and two inside-forwards that took me through my refereeing days from the 30s to the 60s was buried for good. It would be fun if someone brought it back again, but it would be a brave manager.

Because I was close at hand to so many great players in the 40s and 50s people have often asked me what I think about modern football. Well, it is faster now than when I refereed and some of the skill level is very high and players are undoubtedly much fitter and much better athletes. But that doesn't always make the game more open or entertaining and there is so much pressure on managers to win that they often play safe, which can give the crowds or the television viewers boring matches.

To be honest cricket holds more interest for me nowadays, and it was wonderful to see Sussex win the County Championship for the first time in their history in the 2003 season. Cricket has good memories for me, too, of the County Ground and Sussex Cricket Club. This year I had the pleasure of meeting the talented Sussex skipper Chris Adams at a charity dinner I organised in 2003, so I was delighted that Chris, who is a great bloke, led his team to the title.

It was good to see those marvellous scenes from the County Ground (on Thursday 18 September 2003) when the team took the points they needed from Leicestershire after Murray Goodwin scored that crucial four boundary as part of his amazing record innings of 335 not out in the match. I would love to have been there at the County Ground, and what a sight that was on television.

Sussex are the oldest club in the championship (they were formed in 1839) and I wondered if I'd ever see them take the title, so you can imagine how I felt. Well done Chris Adams and his team, from one of their oldest supporters. They had been talking about a top three place at the start of the summer but did even better and I am glad I was around to see it.

They are gentler memories from cricket than football, I suppose. Nowadays cricket seems a much more civilised game than football, and it is more subtle in its skills and tactics. Maybe that is why a lot of people don't watch it now. They have short attention spans and less patience as they rush around and football is more aggressive and instant, but often less satisfying.

As far as I am concerned, there is too much aggression from the players, fans, and the media around football nowadays. Maybe there is too much money involved, too much at stake. Everyone seems to be jumping on the bandwagon and milking the game of football at top level. There are too many overpaid footballers, football writers and commentators, and that seems to have sprung up since the 60s.

There are probably some greedy agents as well but, despite all that, there are still some good matches. At the other end of the scale there are hundreds of thousands playing on the parks for next to nothing or even paying to play. As someone said to me a while back, football seems to survive despite itself.

They have tinkered about with cricket, with this day and night stuff and people prancing around in pyjamas and I hope that cricket survives too. I suppose all sport has to change with the times, as long as they don't squeeze the spirit out of it. One cricket treat I will never forget happened when I was young, during cricket week at Horsham, when Arthur Gilligan was captain of Sussex. We knew if we got to the back of the pavilion the players would come out because their cars were always parked at the back.

I was a very shy boy when I was young and wondered what to say when Arthur came out. He did not know my name, of course, and he asked if I would get something or other out of the car. So I plucked up courage and I said: "I suppose there is no way you would ever talk to a school, sir?"

Arthur said to my astonishment: "Well, if you give me a ring I will see what I can do."

Arthur was a giant of cricket standing before me, and I felt like I had scored a century myself with him talking to me. What a catch, I thought as I prepared to tell my school. Arthur is famous today as much for what he did working for Sussex County Cricket Club as for what he did playing. But he was really some cricketer at his peak.

Arthur took six wickets for seven runs against South Africa in 1924 at Edgbaston, which was thought to be the shortest ever Test innings recorded at 45 minutes and 30 runs. His partner in crime that day was Maurice Tate another Sussex player, and shortly before then in another match the pair of them had skittled out next-door county rivals Surrey for 53.

Arthur was good enough to captain England in two Test series in the middle 20s and he scored a lot of centuries for them. But I think he took a ball on the heart in a game at the Oval and it was said he was never quite the same player again, but he was a tremendous servant to the County Ground for many years. His name must have lasted, you know. He died in 1976 and I am told they even named a road after him in Burgess Hill in the last years of the 20th century at the suggestion of the town council, so there is no doubt he is still remembered.

It was a small honour maybe, but it showed Arthur Gilligan's name lives on and of course has a stand named after him at Hove. Arthur was regarded as a friendly man, and he tried his hand at writing and broadcasting. Anyway at that game at Horsham, in the days when players were almost gods before us because there was no television to make us over-familiar, I overcame my shyness and awe and I dashed back on my bike.

Breathlessly and bursting with pride, I told my sports master that Mr Gilligan would come up one morning after prayers and talk to us. I do not think he believed me but it absolutely made me a hero at the school and I have followed Sussex ever since, and was a member for a long time.

Thumbing through my dozens of old football programmes and my scrap books I came across some things that show the changes in the game, for example the bad affect of not having substitutes.

I remember the fuss that was made when they were brought in long after I retired, but I bet Jimmy Hill would have been glad of one in a game I refereed 50 years ago.

Jimmy, who my son Rod and I have met through charity work, seems to have been sorely missed when Fulham drew 1-1 with Leicester in September 1953.

The following week's programme for the Leeds home match praises the defence for holding out and says: "Their second half performance was particularly praiseworthy because they were weakened by the absence (sic) of Jimmy Hill. " Actually, Jimmy was not missing but he might just as well have been, because he was hobbling painfully on the pitch because of injury.

In those days there was no chance of a substitute and it was not unusual for a quite badly injured player to limp in the forward line just to keep eleven on the pitch. The problem was it often only made their injury worse because being good professionals they would try to stretch for a ball if they thought it would make a difference.

Anyway in this game to accommodate Jimmy Hill's injury a certain Bobby Robson, was moved back to right half so Jimmy could limp at inside-right, but in the days 50 years ago of no substitutes Jimmy ended up limping on the left wing vacated by Charlie Mitten. Robson, of course, went on to manage England and in the later stages of his career has become a well-loved manager of Newcastle United, somewhat restoring their fortunes in recent years.

They talk about clubs selling players because they are "skint" nowadays, like Albion selling their top scorer Bobby Zamora to Spurs this year. But in the 50-51 season Jimmy Hill (to Fulham) and Ron Greenwood (to Chelsea) both had to be sold because Brentford were financially on their knees even though their crowds were about 20,000.

When you think about it, the fans were the ones that lost out back in the 1950s and 1960s when teams lost players during a game or tried to get them to play on through injury. It ruined the match, and two examples that spring to mind are Arsenal's cup defeat in 1952 against Newcastle when they lost Wally Barnes, and Manchester United's shock pre-Munich "Busby Babes" defeat at Wembley in 1957, when their keeper Ray Wood was rendered useless by a reckless charge from Aston Villa's McParland.

In between Newcastle had more luck in 1955, an injury working to their advantage on that occasion, winning the Cup after Manchester City defender Jimmy Meadows went off after only about 20 minutes. I don't think the fans of those clubs who paid hard-earned cash to cheer their teams would say they had fair deal, even though I suppose their teams gave their all with a man short. Despite the usefulness of the substitute rule, I would hate to be a fit, young and talented player sitting on the bench, even though some get paid an awful lot for it. But substitutes have been a good thing for the spectators.

Looking at football now, much though the game has brought me great excitement and joy, I do not really like the way it is played now, although it is faster and the skill level is high. I do not like the way the way players almost gloat when they celebrate nowadays. Enjoy the moment, yes, I think they should, but the posing and posturing is a far cry from the modest handshakes of great players like Lawton, Matthews, and James in the 40s and 50s and I believe can incite the more idiotic elements in the crowd.

I think the egos of modern players get the better of them, although not all. Some of them, like Paul Scholes of Manchester United, let their football skills do the talking, though this seems to annoy the television pundits who always want footballers to give witty answers to their questions, which are often pretty mundane anyway, I think.

There is an obsession now with the media in interviewing players and managers, even if they have nothing especially interesting to say. It's as if the hot air matters more than the match, but someone's making a good living out of it, I suppose. People after the war were extremely passionate about football, but having survived the most terrible times of their lives and lost people in the fighting they had much more of a sense of perspective about sport and life. That gradually disappeared as the memory of the war years faded and that generation passed away and maybe with it some of the discipline. The late Liverpool Football Club manager Bill Shankly made that joke about football being more important than life and death. In the 21st century I sometimes think there are people who believe that.

I think true fans care more about what players do on the pitch. Talking a good game never won any team a title from what I remember. Somebody made me laugh recently when they said you could make up a whole team of ex Liverpool players who spouted on television or radio about football.

I sometimes wonder what the ordinary fan scraping a living thinks about players getting paid a small fortune while they are playing, enough to retire on comfortably in some cases, and then getting paid hundreds of pounds for "yak-yak "as commentators when they hang their boots up.

Maybe football is becoming more middle class, I don't know because I can't get to games any more. But I think it costs £30 or more for a ticket for some

Premier games, which makes it hellish expensive for dad to take his son. I will watch some games like the Cup Final, but I don't watch football as much as I used to. It's still a great game, despite everything, but there is still too much cheating. It's what players call being professional although it usually means they are fouling to make up for lack of judgement or skill.

It's easy to be moral about fouling and cheating, but if a huge bonus or a large chunk of your mortgage payment was at stake I think you might be tempted to trip or block someone who had made you look an idiot by dancing past you with the ball. Players at top level are crafty at trying to hide tripping and blocking, and it is often impossible to tell in a split second whether or not a player has made a genuine mistake in trying to play the ball.

You often hear managers ranting on for television viewers about teams playing with only nine a side if they stick to the letter of the law. That seems to me as if they are saying there should be one set of rules for professionals and another for parks players, which of course would be ridiculous. Only recently a manager on a panel was trying to say a player who deliberately and crudely tripped a player didn't deserve a booking. Why not? It's a long time since I have refereed but believe me, up close professional football is a different world to local stuff. It's a lot more ruthless, and the speed of play can be dazzling if you are out there amongst it.

The great George Best endured appalling treatment, and I remember Pele being hacked out of one World Cup. Today the best forwards like Henry of Arsenal, Giggs of Manchester United, and Owen of Liverpool who would otherwise tear defences to pieces, are regularly fouled to stop them. Yes, people forget that professional football is business, and a hard, sometimes brutal business, even if it does still produce wonderful moments of skill and drama for crowds.

It's wishful thinking to hope cynical, deliberate fouls will ever stop, but it would make the game much more exciting and flowing if they ever did. Football will always be a physical game, that's part of its passion. But deliberate fouling is against the rules. It's as simple as that, though you wouldn't think so to hear some managers and players.

Players have always tried for penalties and blocked runs with obstruction on the blind side of referees, but the foreign players over here have introduced more diving for penalties, which should be stamped on, and too many players are still not punished for deliberate obstruction and blocking. It may not always be dangerous but it ruins the game and denies the advantage to skilful players, and that is not good for the crowds.

Players also have feigning serious injury down to a fine art, and lay there for what seems like half an hour. The problem is that if referees booked players for every "professional foul", block, shirt pull, ankle tap, and the rest we would be watching depleted sides every game, perhaps even worse than those moaning managers suggest.

That's the reality of professional football. Stop your opponent any way you can if you can get away with it. Watch a game closely if you want to see what I mean. No way would I like to be a referee now. It is a different job entirely. They are not respected. I mean, I made mistakes, including some bad ones no doubt, but it was accepted and after the initial protests of players and a bit of a dig in the papers everything moved on.

Now people sitting there with endless video replays in slow motion hammer referees again and again on the television, radio and in the papers. Then they are chewed off again in radio phone-ins. And sometimes they even dig it up again a few weeks later to fill a space. People who mostly wouldn't know how to referee a cubs football match crucify the refs. I think a lot of it is really to do with television ratings and newspaper sales, but that's life today, looking for someone else to blame, and I suppose you have to get on with it.

Just think about it, though. A referee has a split second to make a decision. An armchair expert can slow it down and repeat it until viewers are sick of watching it. How fair is that to a referee? Despite all this, football still produces great moments of magic, and when that happens I suppose we forget all the skullduggery both off and on the pitch. People still love the game, for all its faults.

In the days when things were just as tough but not quite so serious, we had some fun off the pitch with the Evening Argus Quiz Team.

I cannot remember all the names now, it was back in the 50s, but I remember Tommy Farr, the boxer, Arthur Gilligan, the Bedser brothers. I do not think there was any fee, nothing like that. We always had one or two Albion players, and Jack Arlidge was a very good master of ceremonies. Jack was a fine sports reporter and writer and was much respected.

One unexpected result of my travelling around doing matches was that my son Rod, who often went with me, never worked up any great allegiance for any particular club. The Albion played an unwitting part in deciding which club he would follow for the rest of his life, though not in the way perhaps I would have hoped for. One Saturday young Rod announced that whichever team scored the most goals that afternoon he would support forever.

As it happened, a very good Middlesborough side were playing the Albion before about 20,000 people and they crashed six goals past Albion at the Goldstone with future Brighton manager Brian Clough scoring a hat-trick. That proved the biggest score of the day, and Rod still follows the fortunes of Middlesborough in their smart new stadium in the Premier Division. It's a pity the score wasn't reversed though. I always thought the 6-4 win for

Middlesborough at the Goldstone on 20 December 1958 was a lousy Christmas present from Brian Clough and highlights were even shown by the BBC.

One of the Albion scorers that exciting but cruel day was Dave Sexton, a rather shy modest retiring man in the mould of today's Paul Scholes of Manchester United, who later managed top clubs including Manchester United. One of the other Albion scorers, speedy Welsh left winger Freddie Jones, had the unique experience, in my memory at least, of twice being transferred to two different clubs within a year in a job lot with same player.

Jones and Ronnie Clayton had joined Albion for a joint £5,000 fee for the 1958-59 season from Arsenal, but the pair had only left Hereford eight months earlier for Highbury. Jones was popular and skilful but left in 1960 after losing his place to Bobby Laverick and after playing for other clubs gave up League football at only 26, returning to Hereford. In that mauling by Middlesborough another new season signing Johnny Shepherd scored twice, and he finished top scorer with 17 goals before losing his place and leaving.

Deadly Brian Clough, who was of course later to become briefly and controversially Albion's manager with Peter Taylor, was certainly a real jinx on the Albion in that 1958-59 season, after Albion had just been promoted for the first time to the Second Division. In Albion's opening game of the campaign, on the infamous 23 August 1958, he had hammered five past young stand-in keeper Dave Hollins at Ayresome Park, as Albion were thrashed 9-0. Just how cruel football can be, though, was shown when four years later ligament damage ended Clough's career. He later of course won the European Cup as a manager and many other honours.

Browsing through my dozens of programmes and my scrap books they often reveal something of the sports politics and attitudes of the period. When I did Wembley v Uxbridge in the Corthinian League on 6 April 1957, there was certainly a Corinthian spirit about one of the players who missed the match.

When I picked up the programme, which I have kept, it said: "At right back Cyril Webb re-appears and thanks are due to that great sportsman Arthur Percy, who has stood down to give Cyril an opportunity of his showing his paces at back in the first eleven" Somehow I couldn't see that happening in today's football.

One of the goalkeepers I greatly admired was Bert Trautmann of Manchester City who unfortunately did suffer some abuse after the war because of his German family line, despite the fact that he was a smashing bloke. When I officiated at a Portsmouth match in April 1956 the programme noted to my delight: "It is refreshing to see that at long last the barrier has been broken and the genius of Bert Trautmann has been accepted." I was so pleased for Bert, who was a great man.

At the time I thought there was very much a military and naval air about Pompey. Its president was Field Marshall The Viscount Montgomery of Alamein as he was billed on the programme, and the front of the programme boasted "Portsmouth-The Home of HMS Victory."

When I turned up for the Southhampton-Southend Division Three South game professional clubs were complaining bitterly about losing so much money to entertainment tax. Southampton pointed out that they had lost £2,269 in 1953-54 and had handed over £10,901 in entertainment tax. More to the point they reminded supporters that no other sport paid this tax. On top of this the club's rates were being doubled.

Even then clubs were talking about having to rely on bringing through young players instead of buying, an idea Manchester United had developed and which had looked like paying off big time until they lost most of the Busby Babes in the Munich air crash and had to start again, spending a fortune later to buy star replacement players like Denis Law and Albert Quixall.

10   HORSHAM THE GREAT HORNETS

As I left the peak of refereeing well behind me in the 60s and 70s I later got interested in helping my home town team Horsham, who needed a bit of a lift.

There was a businessman called Bernie Newman who I think is the finest businessman I have ever worked with. Horsham Football Club were in pretty bad strokes, and they were at Queen Street where they are still now. The idea was to have a board and Bernard was its chairman. It was the first time Horsham had had a board and it went really well, with weekly draws that brought in money. Bernard was an entrepreneur he made a million or so by selling a brickworks.

Bernard bought an old brickworks and a farm, turned it into a garden centre, and then sold it for tremendous money. He was an absolutely brilliant man and a great pal of mine. We ran the board for several years and pulled things together. And then we said that Queen Street was too awkward for traffic. The council was going to build Broadbridge Heath sports centre and a special ground for the football club.

But no, the old boys on the committee voted against. They said it was too far out of Horsham. Well, we decided we could put on free buses, because it would be only about two and half miles from Horsham to the new ground. Look at it today with some of these grounds, miles from the towns. At any rate, it was turned down and Broadbridge Heath Football Club took it. And we decided to disband the board. All our work had been for nothing. And after that they just went back to the old boys trying to run it. I didn't stay on. I said: "Bugger it."

Current Hon. Sec. and director at Horsham Football Club Jeff Barratt said about this controversy for Knight of the Whistle: "There was a bit of an issue between the board and the management committee about this. One of the issues was that because of complicated tax problems including the Capital Gains Tax and the Land Betterment Levy by the time we had sold Queen Street and acquired the land for the new ground there would only have been sufficient to pay for only changing rooms and a pitch and a not a proper stadium to meet the standards of a semi-professional club. I don't recall there was any particular issue about transport. The key issue was one of economics.

"I don't think there was any particular animosity when they left. I think they felt they had taken things are far as they could and it was time for someone else to take over.

"It is true there was certain amount of friction between the board and the committee but since then they have got much closer together. Certainly, there was a lot of emotional feeling about the prospect of moving out of Queen Street. A lot of people had been going there for years and would have been very upset about any move out of town."

Behind all this, Horsham had a proud heritage of the strongest non-league team in Sussex at one time. They twice reached the first round proper of the FA Cup in the days when it was a cherished competition. As far back as season 1947-48 they fought their way through to play Notts County.

The time 3.01 pm on 29 November 1947 was a glorious moment for the travelling Horsham fans. The hordes of Hornet followers were delirious when Horsham shocked everyone by taking an early 1-0 lead in front of about 23,000 fans after 90 seconds. Ron Smallwood, Horsham's outside left, created a sensation when he scored with a left foot drive. Even the Horsham fans gaped in disbelief for a split second before going wild with delight.

The news was quickly telephoned through for evening paper editions. But one of the greatest centre forwards in English history soon had them re-writing the headlines. Third Division County had just shaken the football world with their signing of the deadly England striker Tommy Lawton for the huge fee (in those days) of £20,000 from Chelsea. Sadly for Horsham, Lawton celebrated his debut with a hat-trick revealing the yawning gap in class as County stepped up a gear, imposed their superior status, and thrashed Horsham 9-1.

For County, Sewell matched Lawton with his own hat-trick, Marsh weighed in with two, and Freeman was the other scorer as the Hornets dream faded and died far from cosy Queen Street. At least the sporting home crowd had the grace to applaud the courage and hard work of Horsham, but it was a long trip home for even the most philosophical Hornets fan. Somewhere in a dusty vault there is a British Movietone film of this match, showing its main star Lawton shaking hands with Horsham skipper Hughes. It would make fascinating viewing if it could ever be found.

The Beatles were in their full pomp by the time my town's team got another crack at a league side in the Cup, in the 1966-67 season. This time the full glory of a national television service reported the match instead of people huddling into a small cinema to watch newsreel film as in 1947. Television was approaching its saturation residency in the corner of the front rooms of the nation and England's World Cup win in 1966 under my old acquaintance Alf Ramsey had fired enthusiasm for televised football.

Queen St was packed with every inch of space that FA Cup day when a packed crowd of 8,000 witnessed the visit of Swindon. Horsham put up stronger resistance this time, and Swindon did not possess any player approaching the massive talent of Tommy Lawton, but the Hornets still went down 3-0. At least Horsham had the consolation of a record crowd.

The club that I followed the fortunes of was first started on a serious footing in 1871 (there had been an informally-run club about ten years before) and eventually proved to be the most successful in Sussex in the years leading up to the Second World War and in those just after it. Horsham truly dominated the 30s in Sussex non-league football and continued their success post-war. They were truly giants of the game for a long period in the county.

Those two "romantic" brushes with league opponents in the FA Cup perhaps exposed the gap between the best amateurs of Sussex and the tough and fitter professionals. But Horsham deservedly won the County League title in 1932, 33, 35, 36, 37, and 38 and it was not unusual for 100 goals a season to be netted by the side. In their own standard they were a class apart. Only Burgess Hill have ever matched this fantastic run of County league titles and they too, bravely, took a path to more senior football, leaving the County League in 2003.

When the County League got back to serious football in 1946-47 Horsham resumed normal service, taking the title again, a masterful achievement bearing in mind the intervening war years wrecked any pattern they had established pre-war. Modern day complaints from teams about being bogged down by cup runs raise a smile from anyone able to remember Horsham's cup exploits post-war. They had already won the Sussex Senior Cup in 1934 and 1939 and then took it again in 1950 and 1954 and their brave runs in the Amateur Cup, then a top-ranking contest that pulled in crowds of about 5,000 to Horsham, thrilled their supporters.

Horsham then won the Metropolitan League in the first season they entered it in 1951, and stalwarts believed that they would have won many more league titles but for getting bogged down by their cup exploits. The club has moved on through the Corinthian League, which it joined in 1957, and the Athenian League, which it joined in 1963 and won in 1973 to the Isthmian League, collecting the Sussex Senior Cup again in 1972, 74, and 76. After all these years the team is still playing at Queen Street and I wish them every success in the future because it is important for Horsham to have a good standard of football to offer fans.

Lots of people who visit me in my old age ask who the greatest players I ever saw were over the years. It is easy to forget and not give due credit but I think, as I said briefly earlier in the book, the best all-round player who I ever saw was

Alex James of Arsenal without doubt. George Cox, the old Arsenal player, had played for Horsham and had a benefit match at Horsham, as I mentioned before. James played for the first half and Arsenal won 4-1. He had come out of retirement and was obviously not at his peak but even then his wonderful skill was obvious.

Jimmy Langley was to my mind one of the finest players for Brighton in the 50s and I should imagine one of the best they have ever had. He was a clever ball player, very clever. He would do well in the game now. He was a jokey player, had a sense of humour. I thought he made the jump from playing for Guildford in the Southern League to the Football League well. I think the crowd loved him because as well as skill he had great spirit.

I wasn't a great surprise to me that Jimmy did so well with Fulham and played for England a few times, he was very talented. Everyone seemed to remember Jimmy for his long throw, but there was more to his game than that. When the great Stanley Matthews was nearing retirement he spoke of how much he looked forward to his duels with Langley. Jimmy was that good.

Later when I was no longer refereeing but keeping an eye on Albion's fortunes I liked the look of the defender Mark Lawrenson. He never seemed to be under pressure and he was probably the classiest defender they have had, although Norman Gall was a fine centre half in the 60s, a marvellous jumper, really got some air between the grass and his boots, and he tried to use the ball well. Lawrenson was sold to Liverpool for £900,000 in 1981 having cost Albion just over £100,000 four years earlier and became one of their finest-ever defenders and later a football commentator.

The two Wilson brothers, Joe and Glen, they were nice guys, I did both their benefit matches, and of course all those marvellous players I mentioned right at the start of my story like Mercer, Carey, Byrne, Edwards, and Wright and John Charles stay in the memory.

It's not all stars that keep football alive, though. Far from it, as I have seen at countless small clubs over decades. There were some good people I came across working for the game at grass roots level over the years, people who never made the papers. Nothing they did was exciting enough to make headlines, but make no mistake the future of football still depends on them. They have marked out the pitches, put up their own nets, ran around picking up players, begged them to pay their "subs" and tried to raise money for clubs for decades.

Without them and the players who pay to play and love the game, football would die. But because of them it never will. And that is true whatever happens to the professional game.

Local football brought me some lively social occasions again organised by those hard-working people I have just talked about.

As later president of the Horsham and District Referees association I chaired the annual dinner in the 60s and one of guests was the late Dr John O'Hara, who did a great deal of work for football and was a familiar figure at functions and trophy presentations. Dr John, as he was affectionately known at grounds, was president of the Sussex County Football League from 1957-1984 a period in which the county made tremendous strides.

A lot of the unpaid officials have served a long time. I was interested to see many years ago, as a referee, that his successor was the equally hard-working Peter Strange, from Burgess Hill, who hopes to complete 20 years as league president next year, 2004. Peter is a former referees secretary and former secretary who has grass roots experience of football from his days as treasurer with the successful Worlds End Football Club, which merged in 1969 with Burgess Hill, then in the County second division, to eventually make the championship-winning Burgess Hill Town side.

The present fixtures secretary Peter Bentley, a retired air traffic controller, also from Burgess Hill, has also served a long time and there are many more like them in the game. That sort of continuity is important as the game progresses but it will be important for new blood to come along and take over.

These are just a few of the many hundreds of people who have helped Sussex football make progress in the past fifty years or so, acting as officials at senior levels and many of them have been what you would call unsung heroes for no pay who didn't get much praise either. Without people like them more than two million footballers nationally would be following their wives and girlfriends around a supermarket or the shops every Saturday or Sunday or finding something else to do instead of playing their favourite sport, and players should never forget that.

As football played a smaller part in my later years, especially in my mid 60s and 70s I concentrated on running the business. I tried to keep my links with cricket, and I was a member at Hove for many years and Joy was as well. I gradually had less and less to do with the business side of the firm, although for many years I did repairs to the table in my workshop at home and liked to keep an eye on things.

I was proud to be chairman of the Sussex County FA for the maximum one year in 1961-62 and served on its council, and was chairman of the referees committee as well as secretary of the Horsham referees Association. As chairman of the Horsham Football League I helped in the merger with the West Sussex League in 1971, although the talks started about a year before. In 1970, my fears over the possible adverse effect on Horsham's local footballers of the neighbouring Crawley New Town led me to propose on behalf of the Horsham Football league its historic merger with West Sussex.

For many years Horsham Football Club had been most successful and they did so much. Not only did they do so well as a football club but they thought the running of a healthy Horsham and District Football League was an advantage to them, because they could see the prospect of more local players coming through the ranks. The West Sussex League was also attracting some works teams from Crawley, who at the time had their own grounds, so they were not paying for council pitches.

One problem faced by Horsham league teams was that even if they were in the top division the League had no Intermediate status and they would have to change to another league, such as West Sussex, to attain intermediate status. This immediate benefit of intermediate status helped sell the merger idea to Horsham League clubs, although it did not meet with unanimous approval.

It actually caused quite a stir when we joined up with the West Sussex League, but it made the best league ever in Sussex and all the county would agree on that. I remain a life member of the West Sussex league. At one time the Horsham league faced a major problem when an official, who we shall not name here alhough I know who he is, began taking money from the league. I believe about £1500 was involved, which was a lot of money in those days.

I got the committee all up to my house and out came the money. He was a nice bloke, a good committee man, but he was gambling. The committee members were all sitting around the table, I will never forget it. He came in, put his suitcase on the table, and said: "Here you are. I am finished. Do what you like."

And that got him away from Horsham. He left, he got the sack. We got it all back. It was never reported to the police, and it never really made the papers. We tried to keep it all quiet, though it was the talk of the town. He was a popular man in the town, especially with bookies, because he couldn't resist a bet. I had the same problem with bar billiards for charity money, when the secretary took several hundred pounds.

I am proud of the small part I played in putting Sussex football on the map, but it was not just me. There have been so many people over the decades, and you know some of them barely get a mention in the press. They were just working at the game they love as well as doing full time jobs. That is what keeps football going, you know. These people, club secretaries, fixtures secretaries, linesmen, and local referees.

Slogging away season after season, sometimes without their teams winning a thing. It may not make the headlines like Brighton and Arsenal and all the rest but football would be finished without these people. It is something I feel very strongly about, this grass-roots love that generation after generation has for football, whatever changes there are in society.

Professional football might destroy itself or go part-time if it gets too greedy or kills public interest in attending games with too much television coverage. But whatever happens ordinary people will always keep the game alive.

I suppose you could say pre-war Sussex football was like Cinderella. Now it is linked in and really run professionally. We have got top men running it, whereas we were a lot of farmers and people like that, workmen, it's amazing. It is 50 times better, but we owe a debt to those who laid the foundation.

I think it really is possibly the best-run county in the country for football. They are brilliant. They really are.

We all worked hard, but we all had jobs, and now it is professional. You have officers based at their own headquarters at Lancing, and their own football pitch. Really, I take my hat off to them, I think they have done a wonderful job. Getting the Sussex County FA headquarters set up at Lancing was a big step forward. Of course, everyone resented it on the council, but I did not. I could see we were going adrift. They thought they were the cat's whiskers and lost their jobs, well most of them did, although people like Ron Reeve stayed and did a great job.

People often ask me if ex-pros would make good referees. I think it helps tremendously if referees have played the game, but not necessarily at the top level. I do not know about recruiting ex professionals, because they are too old really. That is their trouble, they are too old when they finish. Some don't finish until they are 36 or even more nowadays when you look at people like David Seaman is in his 40s now and still playing Premier Division football with Manchester City after a wonderful career with Arsenal and England.

It's a long ladder to get up, you know, a hell of a long one. I was just lucky, I started early. The other problem is that most of the top players are millionaires in their 20s. They don't need the hassle of refereeing and certainly don't need the money, so there is little incentive for them. Jimmy Hill, who of course lives near Hurstpierpoint now, was a player I came across very early in his career who would have made a good top class referee.

Apart from his playing career Jimmy was a bloody good referee, and he did one game when they needed a linesman at Highbury, and he got a lot of acclaim for that the way he handled the job. He would have made a marvellous League referee. He passed the exam, it is a shame more players did not, although quite a lot of them did.

For my book Phil Dennett asked Jimmy Hill for me what he thought of this idea and Jimmy said: "Many years ago I actually came up with a system where apprentices and young players had instruction in the laws of the game and refereeing. Whether they took exams or not was irrelevant to me, because as least it showed they had been taught the laws of the game.

"The problem with professionals becoming referees is that it simply takes them too long to get there. The regulations make sure that professional players won't emerge. It takes too much to get on the conveyor belt.

"Even a player of some intelligence who knows his laws and could handle a game would take about six years and that is nonsense. I have spoken to someone in the game who is very authoritative about this, and they say with professional players it could be done in a year.

"But they do not want to upset the system of referees coming up through the local leagues, they need to retain the incentive of them perhaps reaching

Football League or Premier League status. All they are worried about is keeping people happy at the lower levels because they have more than a million people playing in local leagues."

I actually started the referees association at Horsham with the help of a chap called Joey Richardson. He was centre forward for Horsham for many years and a class one referee. We started it and within a very short time we had got 30 referees, every referee in the villages around Ockley and Rusper, and we were really the start of the Sussex referees association.

I sometimes came across well-known footballers unexpectedly and far away from the playing field.

Jimmy Greaves, there was a brilliant player, but of course another one with a drink problem.

When Jimmy stopped playing after his great career that included Tottenham and England we used to meet in a pub in Lancing, The Crabtree, about every seventh week. Jimmy, you see, was running a business of importing and he used to have lunch at this pub and meet me there. Tarratt's tables had three bar billiards tables there, so I was calling in there from time to time.

Jimmy always seemed to have a new car, I remember once he turned up in a convertible, a lovely car. Every time the kids would turn up to see what car he had. He was living in London at the time, he ran things with his son. However, he has disappeared off the earth now, which is shame because he was brilliant on the box on the Saint and Greavesie show, which was a while back now but was a good programme that I enjoyed a lot.

Of course Jimmy loved driving fast cars and he used to do rallies, He went abroad doing it and he drove to the World Cup I think in Mexico. But he drank like a fish. I was pleased to hear he was booked on the chat circuit recently at Haywards Heath, plugging his new book. Jimmy seems to be looking after himself a little better than George Best. I think Best, fantastic player though he was, seems to be heading for self-destruction if what we read in the papers about his battle with the booze is true. I hope I am wrong.

Another great personality I came across in footballing circles later in life but on this occasion nowhere near a stadium was the comedian Norman Wisdom. He had a house at West Chiltington that was right next to the local football pitch, literally just over the fence. I went along with Joy to represent the Horsham League to the football team's celebration after they had just won a trophy. The club first played league football in 1923, and they were celebrating their latest triumph with great style. Anyway, there was Norman in great form and everyone had a great time.

Norman played and sang for them for three hours solid, trumpet, piano, singing, he was good at everything. What an evening it was. Norman, who was on the Brighton and Hove Albion board at one time, also helped me in football, by introducing me to the right people. He was good to me that way.

Over the years people have asked me what makes referees tick and what makes some better than others.

Well looking back, I thought one of my advantages, and some people might not think of it as such at first, was that my reactions were rather slow. In my case, this gave me a few more seconds to assess and realise what was actually happening. The other thing was also a delaying factor that had the same effect but was something you might not think of. I always held the whistle in my hand when I was doing a game.

Some referees had their whistle constantly in their mouth, and they blew instantaneously when they saw something, or thought they saw something. But because I had the whistle in my hand it took me a few precious seconds to blow and that gave you time. Maybe that helped, it's just a thought I have looking back. I kept fit as a referee, which is an absolute "must," especially I should think in the modern game, which is very quick.

Perhaps that fitness also helped me in everyday life because I have kept pretty nimble over the years, although I think the climbing accident I had in the Army that I told you about had something to do with the pretty bad arthritis I have to live with now. In recent years the lovely house I had at Southwater, where my youngest daughter Kim and her family now live happily, became too much for me and I am now well looked after at the Ashtonleigh home in Horsham, where the family and friends keep in touch.

I was lucky that I stayed fit enough to stay involved in the bar billiards business until I was 78, although not in a big way at that stage of my life as Rod was now running it. In my later years I concentrated on repairing tables and I used to go along to start the finals, because we had finals all over the place, Brighton, Horsham, everywhere. That is where Rod came in.

When I gave the business to Rod in 1987, pool had just come in from America and all the landlords would say they'd had a bar billiards table for years could they have a pool table and said they were going to keep both, which worked to our advantage because of the leagues that sprang up. It really worked in Rod's favour a lot, he really got cracking on it and got pool tables everywhere.

So many years after I first started the tables business it is good to see it still going and providing a living from its base at Oakendene Industrial Estate, Bolney Road, Cowfold, although there are so many counter-attractions now and who knows what the future will hold for any business because things change so quickly nowadays.

Talking of business, one of the greatest men I have known is the late Sir Norman Longley, who once headed the Longley building company. He was a great mate of mine, and I remember one day he took me to Malthouse Road in Crawley and pointed to a house and said: "Ralph, that's where the new hospice is going to be built." And it was. He gave the land and it opened in October 1982, and was built by another Sussex firm that was well known then, Hiltons at

Haywards Heath. Sir Norman became vice-president of the Hospice, which is still doing great work.

11   LUCKY IN LIFE

As you have read in the past chapters, I have had a lot of joy during my long life and, just like everyone else, a share of heartbreak.

I have been married three times, and each of the women in my life had a different attraction for me and had her own special qualities that brought us together. My first wife Billie was young when we married on 28 May 1936, and as you have read things did not work out well in the end. But we enjoyed some good years together until the war brought problems, then we divorced on 13 January 1947, and she moved away from the area.

Billie, born in 1912, died at the age of 90 in September 2002 as this book was being prepared, proving to be the longest surviving of my three wives. The old grocery store we once ran together at Park Street, Horsham, before moving to the Ridgeway, Horsham, became Fennells jewellers and is still there.

It was a tragedy that both my second and third wives, who were such fine women, should fall victim to cancer and be denied many more years of their lives. My second wife Edith was a Bognor girl who I married after her divorce and soon after the divorce of Billie and me in 1947, and she had two young sons Mick and Peter. Under the legal ruling then, Mick went to the Ridgeway with Edith and I, and Peter stayed with his father, while Billie, who moved away from Horsham, had custody of Sonia and Wendy, who were put into boarding school during the war.

I recall first courting Edith at a dance in Feltham but her sons recall I may have actually met her first in the Royal Oak at North Bersted when she had popped in their while waiting for a bus. According to stories told to Edith's family she said to a friend at the pub: "He's mine." and she proved to be right. After a brief spell at the Ridgeway our several homes together over nearly 20 years included Bennetts Road, Horsham, then in 1952 a move to "Wendover" in

Worthing Road in the then much smaller village of Southwater. I remember that Edith was a very good dancer, not that I was. We shared an interest in gardening, I loved it especially, absolutely loved it.

Unlike Billie, who had no real interest in football, Edith often came to matches with me, and was usually invited into the boardroom. But Edith certainly had a wonderful reason, the best, for not coming with me when I refereed the annual Horsham trial match at the start of the 1949 season. When I returned home to our home in Bennetts Road I was told my son Rod had been born. As I told the media, what a great start that was to the season.

Incidentally, these public trial matches were common 50 or so years ago, and were reported in the press. I regularly did the Albion trial matches, and sometimes they drew gates of several thousand. They were a useful pre-season warm-up for me, too.

Edith sometimes took Rod along to matches as he grew up so he could see what his dad was getting up to. Occasionally if the crowd really got at me this had its down side. Rod recalls: "I remember at least one game as a youngster when I got very upset about the things the crowd were shouting at my dad. My mum had to take me by the hand out of the stand because I was crying."

Edith was very sociable and she got to know everybody. When I was refereeing Arsenal and Charlton in the 50s she met an actress there and they were friends for years. We shared a lot of good times and we were married for 23 years, the last few years of her life living with me and young Rod at the new bungalow I had built, called "Talsarnau".

The beautiful bungalow stands close to "Wendover," and gets its name in a roundabout way from the struggle I had with the local council to get planning permission to build it. When I received the call saying the planning application had been approved I was staying in a cottage at Talsarnau in Wales and I was so delighted that I named the bungalow after the village.

Earlier, I had bought allotment land on which "Talsarnau" now stands for £50 and had grown crops on it. Rod reminds everyone how one day I announced: "I have found a way to make my first million."

The family likes to recall even now how I hoped to make a lot of money growing blueberries, not least of all because American servicemen, thousands of whom who had been sent to the UK and Sussex, liked blueberry pie.

I had come across them during my spell in the RAF. Fired by enthusiasm I dug up all my potatoes and planted the blueberries. Sadly, they never caught on and Rod recalls I was left with "tons" of them. His verdict after all these years was that they were proved rather too seedy. Another Tarratt money-making idea passed into history, but we were happy enough. My travelling salesman job with the women's clothing was going well and there was a good income from the bar billiards, which by the mid-50s had become Sussex Bar Billiards, before later becoming Tarratt's Tables in 1978, Rod then taking over nine years later.

But then tragedy struck the family when poor Edith got stomach cancer and she was treated in the Royal Sussex County Hospital at Brighton. She took it bravely although it was so distressing for everyone. I took ten months off to nurse her at home but she was beyond help. It was too late, we lost her in March 1964, and it took the family and me a long time to get over that.

Among the items Edith had treasured in her life was a medal given to me by President Peron to commemorate the Argentina and Spain match in 1953, which I have described in detail elsewhere in the book. I went to see Wakefield's the jewellers in Horsham and said my wife would like the medal to be made into a brooch. And he said did I know because of the history behind it that it was worth a hell of a lot of money. It had beautiful stones, unusual stones; I have never seen anything like it.

If I can leap back 50 years to 1953, the strange part was that when we came back from the night-club after Peron presented the medal there were a lot of police cars outside the hotel. I went up to my room to get ready for bed and everything was all over my room. This medal had been stolen. It had gone. We were up all night because the police were about. They tracked it down to the "buttons" in the hotel a chap of about 16 or 17 who had sold it on by the time they found him, and they gave him four years inside. I never got that medal back.

But about three months after we got back to England Sir Stanley Rous rang me and said: "I have a surprise for you." They had made another one for me and Sir Stanley said: "You have got a much better one than they gave you there." It was specially made I suppose. It was later put into a drawer in the house and, sad to say, it later went missing and was never found.

One act of great kindness I recall when Edith was seriously ill was a telephone call from Tommy Docherty, who many people will remember as the former Scotland international and Manchester United manager, who I had come across in my travels as a referee. When he heard about the plight of poor Edith, Tommy offered me his villa abroad, which I thought was a very kind gesture. He has always been full of wisecracks, Tommy, he has this cocky image, but there has always been a good heart there, too. It made the loss of Edith a little more bearable, to know that people cared so much.

I met my wonderful third wife Joy in rather unusual circumstances that might not sound very romantic in one way, but were in another. To be honest, I thought I was in love with another barmaid in the same pub, the Foresters in Kirdford, when I started getting interested in Joy. She had been in secretarial work but was looking for something more interesting, although later her office experience was invaluable to the bar billiards business.

The story the family remembers is that I rang the Foresters asking the other girl for a date and Joy answered the telephone, somehow craftily engineering a date with me. And then this other girl left, and anyway she did not want to know me. Joy must have been the right one for me, and we married about six months after we met, on 12 June 1969, when my best man was Fred Lane, who years before had the thrill of lining at an FA Cup Final.

In January 1971 our daughter Kim was born. Kim was a bright girl academically and her BA Honours studies in leisure marketing led to a placement at Bournemouth Football Club, which she loved, and she did a dissertation on football in the community. Her disappointment was not getting a job with West Ham because it wasn't financially viable. The consolation was that at Bournemouth, where she regularly accompanied the players on social occasions, my daughter met Jamie Redknapp, Robbie Fowler, and Steve McManaman when they enjoyed a night out in Jamie's home town.

Staying in Manchester with a friend she also met Ryan Giggs but reported that his "personality wasn't as exciting as his football skills." Kim certainly kept up the family football connection, meeting Chelsea and Wimbledon stars when she later helped to run 30 night-clubs for First Leisure before accepting voluntary redundancy and settling down to married life and children with Mo after their wedding in 1999.

Well, from the time we married all those years ago Joy and I could not have a made a better life, until she died from cancer in St Catherine's Hospice in February 1999. Her death came only a few months before the family shared the delight of Kim and Mo being married. Joy and I had made our home at the house I had built in Southwater after leaving Bennetts Road. It was built on land next to where I bought a smaller home Wendover previously, and the new house caused a bit of fuss because it was across a path, but it got through the council.

When Joy died it was difficult to believe that I had lost another poor wife to cancer. Joy was a wonderful wife. She looked after me, my books, my money, and she was brilliant. She did all the financial side. I did all the selling and she looked after the figures. Above all that she was a great companion and friend to me. She died from ovarian cancer, which was the same cancer that Eva Peron died from, which I remember from my meeting with President Peron in 1953.

Joy was always good company at social events but she must have wished she had stayed at home one evening when I took her out to dinner. I took Joy for a pub meal at Ockley on her birthday when the actor Oliver Reed, who most people know had a big drink problem, came up and demanded my table. He said he wanted it for his party. I said he could not have it and I thought at that moment he would hit me. He was very unpleasant when he was drunk and my wife and I eventually told the manager we would find somewhere else because we could not stand his noise. We went to the Wheatsheaf where there was a much happier atmosphere. He may have had some talent, but when he was drunk he behaved like a nobody. The blighter had been banned from most pubs in the area.

There were many good times that I hope everyone enjoys with their partners, but when Joy was diagnosed with cancer they were dark days, despite her immense courage. Anyone who lost a loved one to cancer will know what I mean. When Joy fell dangerously ill and there was no hope for her they were absolutely marvellous at St Catherine's Hospice in Crawley. It was just a brilliant place. I could not speak any higher of them.

So that is why I worked with them on fund-raising, until I got the arthritis pretty badly and had to slow down a little. It helped me to get over her death to do something positive, and they do such good work. I was chairman of the Southwater branch of the hospice. I started it after Joy died in 1999, to repay their kindness and dedication and that is why, as I said at the start of this book, I decided to give proceeds of this book to the hospice.

Looking back over nearly ten decades now, I have always believed, whether it is in sporting, personal, or business life, that work and preparation help you succeed. Yet it is a hard fact of life that, however strongly you strive in anything you do, you always need a little luck to come your way now and then. Maybe the football injury that stopped me playing the game I loved at 22 did me a favour, even though I certainly did not feel lucky at the time because playing gave me such a thrill.

I am certain that I would never have played football at anywhere near such a high level as I refereed, because to be frank I was not talented enough. It was easy for me to accept that, working as I was up close with professionals and seeing the demanding standards required of even the humblest of them. Believe me, when they say, as they always do, that it looks a lot easier from the touchline they are 100 per cent right.

It's a cliché, but like a lot of cliches it is true and I suppose it's equally true of refereeing. Out there everything happens faster, there seems less space, your vision of the pitch is narrower. I think that's why the truly great players are those that find time, create space, and seem to have periscope vision over the pitch for spotting other players. I couldn't see me doing that, somehow, however keen I was on the playing the game.

Half a century on, I believe that big break with the whistle at Highbury in 1951 when Mr Law was hurt and I took over in front of Stanley Rous, one of the most influential men in football was the biggest turning point for me as a referee. And thinking of all the friends that died in the Second World War if I had not failed that health medical for the RAF I would have become a rear gunner with all the risk of death that carried, and I almost certainly would not be here to tell my story.

Sport, business, and family have given me great fulfilment surrounded by some of the best friends a man could have, some of whom still keep in touch to this day.

As I reflect in my old age now, if I can borrow a footballing term, I am grateful that most of the big decisions in my long and happy life have gone my way.

RALPH TARRATT OCTOBER 2003

12   TRIBUTES TO RALPH TARRATT

As a postscript to Knight of the Whistle the following people offered their tributes to Ralph. They include a few of the hundreds of people since the 1930s who have admired his devotion to football in Sussex in the cause of the county's referees, without whom the organised game would not have survived into a third century.

Susan Town fund-raising manager at St Catherine's Hospice, Crawley: "Ralph did a lot to help us set up the Southwater fund-raising branch. He had so many contacts and called up many of his friends to help. The group is still thriving and he really did give us a lot of help, and recruited a lot of people to the lottery."

Ron Reeve, from Shoreham, who was Sussex County FA secretary for 30 years said: "Ralph blazed a trail for other Sussex referees, showing them they could aspire to that level of achievement. Anyone who has been connected with Sussex football for any length of time will know the name Ralph Tarratt.

"I am sure he was the first referee from Sussex to referee top international matches. And of course he was the first from the county to make the Football League list. Only five others from Sussex have achieved that honour, Tom Bune, who moved into the county, Michael James, Martin Bodenham, Alan Gunn, and Gary Willard, the last three of which also reached international standard.

"Ralph was on the Sussex County FA council when I joined in 1956. I always remember him as a very engaging man. He had achieved a lot but he was not on his high horse because he had done it all. He was always very modest and measured. Ralph always said if you didn't see the ref he was a good 'un, and even now most people who are involved with referees would agree.

"I never knew that he took up refereeing because of injuries he got playing football. As it happened, it worked to the advantage of both himself and the world of refereeing."

Tony Adfield, from Henfield, who was general secretary of the West Sussex Football League for 13 years and is now its president said: "Ralph wasn't only interested in refereeing, although he was passionate about that. He had football at heart and it was his foresight that brought about the merger of the Horsham League and the West Sussex League in 1971. It was Ralph, who was chairman of the Horsham and District FA, that actually ran the league, and Bill Saunders, of the West Sussex League who were the prime movers. Ralph could see that clubs in the Horsham League would gradually move away to the West Sussex League. At the same time, he saw that the West Sussex League was having a great deal of trouble with their administration. They were looking towards the Horsham league to provide officers to get them on an even footing.

"Ralph was steeped in the local game and a keen and able administrator. He was a blooming good chairman of a meeting and I was very grateful to him as the new league's general secretary. Ralph was quite capable of dealing with a situation. He was tough if needed, but on the other hand he could be quite humble. I didn't know him as a referee, only as an administrator, and he was very good at that. I was delighted when I was able to present Ralph with his Football Association medal for 50 years service to the game."

Bill Saunders, a fellow referee and former official and president of the West Sussex League says: "In his time Ralph was a pioneer in getting Sussex referees to the right people at the right time so they could progress outside the county. When he first started Sussex was not a very fashionable county in football terms. We had only one professional club in the county, Brighton, and that was only in the Division Three South. Referees were very slow in coming through, and it was very difficult until Ralph came on the scene for our referees to get on to leagues outside Sussex.

"He was able to help because of his progress as a referee. He was pre-war Class One and he was much further on in the field of promotion. Very few

Sussex referees have got on to the Football League list. Because he was in such a position, he was able to help so many people. And that was what he did. Behind the scenes, he helped others. He never thought of himself. There are several people in Sussex football who did get out into other leagues because of him.

"He was able to put people forward. These people had a kind word put in for them in the right quarters without them knowing. He was helping because he knew what a struggle it was. It is like in a football club when a player feels he has to move to make progress because he is not in a fashionable club. The same thing happened in refereeing. Sussex was just not fashionable. We were very much a Cinderella county before the 1950s. Not only in refereeing but in football."

As recalled earlier, Ralph played a leading part in merging the Horsham and West Sussex Leagues.

Bill recalls: "Ralph said there was no reason why the Horsham League could not merge with West Sussex. The reason why it came up rather quickly was that Ralph feared that Horsham with all its history might be swallowed up by the new town at Crawley. The danger he saw was that they might take over the football. That was Ralph's fear and it had no doubt been expressed at one of his Horsham League meetings. The fear definitely was that Horsham local football could be swallowed up by Crawley. The merger was something that he did which brought about a significant change in local football. Quite apart from this he was a great character to have around."

Peter Wilkins, who has known Ralph since he was boy of five buying sweets at the shop Ralph ran with his first wife Billie, had better luck in playing football and went on to play for Horsham and Worthing, later becoming a Class 1 referee and in fact passing his exam at Ralph's home. As a leading official of the

Horsham League he took part in the 1970 negotiations that led to the West Sussex League merger in 1971.

Mr Wilkins, who still keeps in touch with Ralph, said: "Ralph was an excellent administrator, and he was to the fore in everything we did. He had such knowledge of football and he was also intelligent too. On top of that he had great common sense, a lot of people have intelligence but no common sense.

"In the world of refereeing he was very energetic. He was also a very debonair man, he was quite young when he was climbing the refereeing ladder and that helped the image of Sussex refereeing a little because he was also a top class referee.

"He was a youngster when he started and got on very well. He kept going doing his refereeing when he was serving abroad in the war, which helped him when he came to pick up his career after the war.

"But above everything Ralph has always been a good man. Everybody I came across liked him. I know you shouldn't like referees, but they liked Ralph."

Jeff Barratt, former referee, and current Hon Sec and director of Horsham Football Club in 2003 said: "He did some quite outstanding things in his time, being one of the English referees who went out to South America because they wanted to sort out all the corruption there. At local refereeing level he was really wonderful with the youngsters, and used to insist he'd come along to speak at local meetings however busy he was. He was the first Sussex referee to reach the highest level, but there have never been any airs and graces with him."

Shoreham Football Club paid its own tribute to Ralph when he was at his peak. In their programme for the home match with Brighton Old Grammarians on 18 December 1954 the Christmas spirit of goodwill positively shone through. Even then, viewed in the current age of cynicism and regular abuse of referees, the remarks appear remarkably generous. The programme notes said, amongst other things, "One thing we can be certain about. For this match we have been allocated a referee who will make clear-cut decisions and really control the game."

Managers and players, ever since the days when a pig's bladder was belted about a field, have always look for excuses in defeat by blaming someone else. So of course there had to be a sting in the tail of this programme. It goes on: "This alas, is not always the case and one often sees the quality of play deteriorate as a result of silly decisions made by referees."

One of the most remarkable tributes to Ralph, although perhaps a little tonque-in- cheek, came in a letter after he had refereed the Southern League match between Hastings and title-chasing Worcester on 22 March 1952. Hastings lost a dramatic match three goals to two when their forward Rudkin hit the post with a penalty with three minutes left. Ralph had awarded the kick when the visiting goalkeeper Woodward brought down Crowther of Hastings.

Despite the defeat a spectator who knew Ralph sent him a letter four days later, passing on the praise of Hastings supporters. Signing the letter only "Bert" the admirer said: "Believe me, Ralph, if you can please Hastings supporters you are not a marvel but a genius."

BIBLIOGRAPHY

David Miller -*Stanley Matthews*- 1989

John Roberts -*The Team That Wouldn't Die*- 1975

Tim Carder and Roger Harris- *Albion A -Z, A Who's Who of Brighton and Hove Albion FC* -1997

Bryon Butler-*The Football League 1888 to 1988*- edition 1988

Tim Carder and Roger Harris -*Seagulls! The Story of Brighton and Hove Albion FC*- 1993
Bill Frindall- *Guinness Book of Cricket Facts and Figures*- 1987
Chris Taylor- *The Beautiful Game, A History of Latin American Football*-1988
EW Swanton- *Cricketers of My Time*-1999
Jack Rollin- *The World Cup- 1930 to 1990* -1990
Roger Hutchison -*The Toon Complete History of Newcastle United FC*- 1997
Keir Radnedge-*Ultimate Encyclopaedia of Football* -1994
Norman Barrett -*The Daily Telegraph Chronicle of Football*- 2001 edition
Stephen F Kelly -*The Old Trafford Encyclopaedia*- 1993
Phil Soar- *The Illustrated Encyclopaedia of British Football*- 1989
Tom Tyrrell and David Meek -*The Illustrated History of Manchester United*- 2000
Radovan Jelinek and Jiri Tomes- *First World Atlas of Football*-2002

THANKS for information provided personally or through website by: Mark Chapman Brentford FC, Fulham FC, Middlesborough FC, Newcastle FC, Arsenal FC, Horsham Library for film records of West Sussex County Times, Haywards Heath library, Horsham FC and GoatZone website, Ralph Tarratt- club programmes and cuttings albums 1930-1957, FIFA, Argentine FA, Chilean FA, Uruguayan FA, Football Association, Premier League, Nationwide League Media Office, Nick Wisdom, St Catherine's Hospice, Kim Khan (nee Tarratt), Rod Tarratt, Sonia Tarratt, Mick Foskett, Peter Foskett, Sussex County FA, Tony Brown and Association of Football Statisticians.

Thanks also for the assistance of Neil Wallis chief sub editor of the Mid Sussex Times, Steve Wrench, graphic designer, of Sussex Newspapers, and Kim Dennett for help and imagination in design and preparing photographs; Chris Dennett and Alan Needham for copy checking and lots of patience, The Argus, West Sussex County Times, Chatham News and The News, Portsmouth for use of photographs.

Photograph of Ralph Tarratt back cover copyright Steven Dennett 2003. Cover designs by Steve Wrench. Cartoon of Ralph Tarratt by Bob Green

All proceeds from this edition will be given to St Catherine's Hospice at Crawley.